Unexpected New Life

Unexpected New Life

Reading the Gospel of Matthew

MATTHEW J. MAROHL

CASCADE *Books* • Eugene, Oregon

UNEXPECTED NEW LIFE
Reading the Gospel of Matthew

Cascade Books
An Imprint of Wipf and Stock Publishers
199 W. 8th Ave., Suite 3
Eugene, OR 97401

www.wipfandstock.com

ISBN 13: 978-1-60608-797-8

Cataloging-in-Publication data:

Marohl, Matthew J.

Unexpected new life : reading the Gospel of Matthew / Matthew J. Marohl

viii + 98 p. ; 23 cm. Includes bibliographical references.

ISBN 13: 978-1-60608-797-8

1. Bible. N.T. Matthew—Commentaries. I. Title.

BS2575.53 M37 2012

Manufactured in the U.S.A.

To my wife, Sarah
and
To my daughters, Noa and Greta

Contents

1
Unexpected New Life
Identifying a Theme

The Gospel of Matthew tells the story of Jesus. But more than that, from the very first verse through the last, it announces that *from expected death comes unexpected new life.* This theme of hope and promise is woven into the gospel in surprising and powerful ways. The gospel begins with the genealogy of Jesus. Even here, in a long list of unfamiliar names, the author tells four stories of expected death and transformative new life. Immediately following the genealogy is the gospel's first narrative, its first story. In the account of the birth of Jesus, we are challenged with Joseph's dilemma. What is a righteous man to do when confronted with the pregnancy of Mary? This dilemma is one of expected death and unexpected life. As the author continues to tell the story of Jesus, a theme is developed. As readers, we are drawn into situations of expected death and are again and again surprised by the unexpected, the promise of new life.

What Is a "Gospel" and Why Does It Matter?

I invite you to think about a scenario that you have, no doubt, experienced dozens of times. You are planning to watch a movie with a friend and now it is time to select the film. If it is a new movie, and you are going to the theater, you might list movie titles. But, if you are planning to watch an older movie, one that is no longer in the theater, you will likely engage in a discussion centered upon genres. "Do you want to see a romantic comedy? How about a good drama? Or, perhaps we should see a classic horror film?" We are comfortable selecting movies based upon genre because we know (at least roughly) what to expect. At the end of a long workweek we might not "want to think too much," so we go with a comedy. We imagine that it will be light and will set the tone for the weekend. We will save a foreign film with subtitles for another day.

We may not be aware of it, but the role of genre is very important. Genres are important because they tell us what to expect. We are so familiar with genres, and genres are so predictable, that we could write our own genre-specific story. If I asked you to write a romantic comedy, you could do so with ease. Romantic comedies all begin in the same way. Two people meet. Within a few minutes into the movie, we all know exactly what will happen: they will end up together. We get to experience their first date, sometimes awkward, sometimes romantic. Next, we watch the classic "dating montage." Here, we see around a dozen dates in back-to-back, several-second clips all the while listening to an upbeat pop song (here we are at a baseball game, here we are walking at sunset, here we are visiting our families at Christmas). Then we experience the struggle, the tension, the turmoil, the break-up. There is a misunderstanding and, for a few key moments, we are sure that their relationship is over. But, alas, our worries were not warranted. The couple gets back together and we watch them dance or kiss or get married as the ending credits roll and the summer's biggest love song plays. We feel affirmed. Love has triumphed. Importantly, we experienced exactly what we expected.

We could go on and on. Sports movies end with the big game. Slow motion is used during the final play. When the team, *our* team, the underdog, wins, we feel that we have won. Horror movies end with a climactic moment. Or should I say, climactic moments? The bad guy, the monster, the killer, is never killed on the first try. It takes multiple attempts for good to conquer evil. Genres are important, primarily because they let us know before we even begin a story what to expect.

It is only when we are familiar with a genre that we can detect the differences between stories. Sometimes the differences seem insignificant. We might say, "This is the same movie, but the football players have been replaced with basketball players." In some cases, however, the differences make all the *difference*. An idea or theme is introduced into an otherwise familiar genre and we are drawn into the story. How will this romantic comedy play out after one of the central characters dies in the opening scene? The genre is still familiar, but we detect that there is something different, something special about this telling of the story.

As we read the Gospel of Matthew we must ask ourselves similar questions, questions of genre. What is a gospel? What is the genre? This is an important question because it tells us what we can expect. If a gospel were a modern romantic comedy, we would expect romance. If a gospel were a sports film, we would expect a big game. But what can we, what *should* we, expect from a gospel? And, perhaps most importantly, how is the Gospel of Matthew different? What do these differences tell us? After all, it is usually in the subtle differences where the intent of the author, and the beauty of the story, truly lies.

We must begin, then, with the question of genre. What is a gospel? This question is traditionally answered in one of two ways. For some people, the gospels represent a unique literary genre, unlike any other writing at the time. Here, it is argued that the gospels are the written form of the earliest preaching of the church. Followers of Christ in the first decades after the death and resurrection of Jesus shared his important story with one another. This oral process eventually became formalized and finalized in writing. It is this written work that we know as a gospel. For others, the gospels are understood to be similar to first-century biographies. Here, it is believed that if we examine the genre of ancient biography, we will better understand the gospels that we encounter in the New Testament.

So, where does this leave us? Fortunately, the two views regarding the gospel genre do not need to be understood as alternate or opposing positions. It is true that both oral and written traditions informed the writing of the gospels. However, this does not mean that when they finally came to be written they were not also informed by the biographical style common at that time. In other words, the author of Matthew used oral and written traditions to tell the story of the life and death and resurrection of Jesus. Furthermore, the format used to tell this story is similar in many ways to other ancient biographies. Knowing what to expect from an ancient biography, then, will help us know what to expect from a gospel.

For us, two important aspects of ancient biographies will inform our reading of the Gospel of Matthew. First, ancient biographies include sayings, anecdotes, and stories for the primary purpose of revealing the *character* of the individual. As modern readers, we expect biographies to include very specific historical data. We want to know every "who, what, where, and when" possible. It would be unthinkable to write a biography today and not include a complete list of important life events, a detailed list of family members, and a full physical description of the individual. Furthermore, we wish to be provided with emotional and psychological revelations. Why did the individual say and do the things that were said and done? Finally, we expect a sense of "character development." We believe that we are not static in our personalities and that we are shaped (or "made") by our successes and failures. Ancient biographies are, to put it mildly, quite different.

The primary intent of the ancient biography is to express the essential character of the individual. The sayings that are shared, the anecdotes that are relayed, and the stories that are included are all meant to provide insight into the nature of the person being introduced. By our standards, therefore, much is left out. We want "history," in the twenty-first-century sense of the word. But, what we are given are *lives*. Perhaps a most helpful way of understanding the gulf between our expectations and what is provided by ancient biographers is to read a description of the writing process by Plutarch (ca. 45–120 CE). Plutarch, a well-known historian and biographer, tells us that it is his intention to reveal the souls of men, rather than to describe mere deeds.

> It is the life of Alexander the king, and of Caesar . . . that I am writing in this book, and the multitude of the deeds to be treated is so great that I shall make no other preface than to entreat my readers, in case I do not tell of all the famous actions of these men, nor even speak exhaustively at all in each particular case, but in epitome for the most part, not to complain. For it is not Histories that I am writing, but Lives; and in the most illustrious deeds there is not always a manifestation of virtue or vice, nay, a slight thing like a phrase or a jest often makes a greater revelation of character than battles where thousands fall, or the greatest armaments, or sieges of cities. Accordingly, just as painters get the likenesses in their portraits from the face and the expression of the eyes, wherein the character shows itself, but makes very little account of the other parts of the body, so I must be permitted to devote myself rather to the signs of the soul in men, and by means of these to portray the life of each, leaving to others the description of their great contests. (*Alexander* 1)

In short, ancient biographies intend to reveal the character, the nature, of the individual. While sayings, stories, and life events are important, they are only important insomuch as they reveal the true essence of the person. Plutarch notes that some stories are left out. Some stories are only partially told. This should not matter. What matters is that the reader of such a biography glimpses the true individual. Using the words of Plutarch to guide us, consider the intent of an ancient biography to reveal *lives*, rather than to simply tell history.

If the revelation of character is the first of the two important aspects of ancient biographies, the second is the apologetic nature of the works. Do not be tricked by the term "apologetic." This simply means that the work is written with a clear goal in mind. Ancient biographies are written to convince the reader of the importance of the individual. In other words, they have no intention of being neutral. Ancient biographies are written to describe and defend the virtue of the individual. Most modern biographies attempt to be neutral. When we are read a biography of Thomas Jefferson, we believe that the story is being told from a fair, balanced, and unbiased position. We are learning about Thomas Jefferson and not the author. Ancient biographies are "biased" in the sense that they are written to convince readers of the relative value and virtue of the person in question.

So, how will this inform our reading of the Gospel of Matthew? The author of our work intends to reveal the essential character of Jesus. The stories that are told and the sayings that are shared have a clear goal: to reveal the *person* of Jesus. As modern readers, we may wish that other material were included. How old was Jesus when he died? What year was it when he was crucified? But it is not the intention of our author to simply write a history. In the Gospel of Matthew, it is the very *life* of Jesus that is revealed. In addition, this is not a neutral text. The story is told with a purpose. The author wants you to believe that Jesus is the Son of God and that in him and through him unexpected life is more than possible; it is promised.

How Is the Gospel of Matthew Different, Unique, and Why Does This Matter?

Each of the four gospels in our New Testament is different. For some readers, this is a problem to overcome. For others, the differences are intriguing and important. In the section above, we learned that ancient biographies were written to express the essential character of an individual.

Furthermore, these biographies were not neutral. They were written to convince readers of the worth, the virtue, the importance of the individual being described. This is also true with the Gospel of Matthew. The gospel, in a captivating narrative, describes the person, the very *character*, of Jesus. But more than that, the gospel tells readers why Jesus should matter to them. So, why do we have more than one gospel? Reflecting again upon our discussion of genre helps us to answer this question.

If the goal of ancient biographies was to report history (as *we* understand history) some of the differences between the gospels might seem quite problematic. For example, both the Gospels of Matthew and Luke provide genealogies for Jesus (the Gospels of Mark and John do not). As modern readers, we would assume that the lists would be the same; or, very nearly the same. After all, how could they be different? But, the two lists are different, very different. In fact, I challenge you to read both lists and find the *similarities* (or, you can just take my word for it). Both gospels trace the lineage of Jesus beginning with Joseph. However, it is with Joseph that the commonality seems to end. In Matthew's gospel, the father of Joseph is Jacob. In Luke, the father of Joseph is Heli. In Matthew, the father of Jacob is Matthan, son of Eleazar, son of Eliud. In Luke, the father of Jacob is Matthat, son of Levi, son of Melchi. I could go on. While I will discuss the genealogy of Jesus in the next chapter, for now it is enough to point out the differences in the two lists, and to point out that some differences (such as these) are quite difficult to reconcile. Who was Jesus' grandfather on his father's side—Jacob or Heli?

Many of the differences between the gospels, however, *seem* much easier to explain. For example, in Matthew's gospel we are told that when the disciples see the resurrected Jesus, they worship him, but some doubt (28:17). Here, many modern readers are tempted to fill in what we perceive is left out, exclaiming, "Oh, the one who doubted is Thomas!" In other words, we borrow the story of Thomas' doubt from the Gospel of John (20:24–29) to "complete" the story from Matthew. For us, this process seems to kill two birds with one stone. First, we have eliminated the difference between the gospels. Second, we believe that we have filled out and enriched Matthew's story, which was previously short and vague.

Without even thinking about it, we may harmonize the gospels (we push two or more stories together to make a bigger, more "consistent" story). So, what is wrong with harmonizing? At one level, perhaps nothing is wrong with this practice. We don't, after all, know who doubted after the resurrection. So, we might reason that relying upon and blending all four of the gospels is the most complete way of understanding the Jesus story. The practice of harmonization does, however, have a significant drawback. Harmonization eliminates the unique features of each gospel. Furthermore, it is quite often in the unique elements of a story that the author invests meaning. In other words, rather than be threatened by differences and attempt to smooth out or eliminate them, why not ask, "Why did Matthew tell the story in this way?"

Rather than ask, "Why are Matthew and John's genealogies different?," why not ask, "What does *Matthew's* genealogy tell us about Jesus?" Rather than ask, "Why is Matthew's description of doubt different from that in John's gospel?," why not ask, "What does *Matthew's* story tell us about the disciples?" Throughout this book, we will read and consider the Gospel of Matthew. Furthermore, we will assume that the author of Matthew tells this story of Jesus with great care and attention to detail. In other words, the story is told in a particular way for a particular purpose. Previously, we learned that ancient biographies were written to reveal the *character* of an individual. We must ask, then, "What does Matthew's gospel reveal about the character of Jesus?"

I will warn you: you will be very tempted to import details from other gospels into your reading of Matthew. And you will be frustrated at times with my choice of words. For example, I will explain that after the crucifixion, after the Sabbath, Mary Magdalene and the other Mary went to see the tomb (28:1). You may think to yourself, "The other Mary—who is that?" But Matthew does not tell us. I *do* ask that you attempt to read and consider the Gospel of Matthew alone, as a unique telling of the Jesus story. If you do, I believe that you will be richly rewarded. The Gospel of Matthew is different from the other gospels. It begins with a different genealogy and ends with the "Great Commission," a feature that is unique to Matthew. Along the way, we will discover a theme. Throughout the Gospel of Matthew we will learn that *from expected death comes unexpected new life.*

Conclusion Awareness

Many of us have a romantic notion of the first readers or listeners of the gospels. We imagine people who have never heard the story of the life of Jesus. So, they hang on every word. When the disciples and Jesus are in a boat that is being tossed around at sea, the first listeners, we imagine, can feel the tension of the life-or-death situation (8:23–27). Perhaps most importantly, the crucifixion of Jesus brings the listeners into the heart of despair. The resurrection, in turn, brings the same surprise and joy that was experienced by the women who first witnessed the empty tomb. In short, each step of the story is new. Like other stories heard for the first time, the events are thought to unfold and build with a sense of awe and wonder; each step, building upon the last, until the final climatic moments are revealed.

This understanding of a first-time reader carries with it the assumption that the author of Matthew used foreshadowing; that clues were placed in the text to help the reader to anticipate yet unknown events to come. The story of the transfiguration of Jesus, for example, might be understood to be a foreshadowing of Jesus' future resurrection glory (17:1–13). Even Jesus himself foreshadows his own death and resurrection when talking with his disciples (16:21–23; 17:22–23; 20:17–19; and 26:1–2). In each case, we might believe that these acts of foreshadowing are clues embedded in the story, but that the true ending remains ultimately unknown to the reader until it is finally revealed.

I say that this is a "romantic" notion, for there are some stories that cannot be told in a linear fashion, stories that cannot be successfully told from the beginning to the end. Such are stories with a universally known ending, an ending that is already known before the story is even told. A helpful example of this is the story of the Titanic. It is impossible to tell a story about the Titanic without its final hours looming large over the entire story. I cannot tell you about the construction of the ship without you already thinking about its demise. I cannot tell you about the captain or crewmembers or passengers without you thinking about their deaths. Although the story is a century old, it continues to captivate audiences. Its ending ensures that it will be told and retold. And, the ending impacts the telling of every aspect of the story. In fact, it cannot be otherwise.

While telling such a story involves obvious obstacles, it also invites the storyteller to employ a technique that I call "conclusion awareness." The practice of foreshadowing allows the storyteller to offer a glimpse of what is to come; an event that is to come and is unknown to the audience. The practice of conclusion awareness begins with the assumption that the audience already knows the ending. Furthermore, this ending necessarily casts a shadow and impacts the telling of all other events in the story. The story, then, must be told from a unique perspective. The characters in the story do not know the ending, but the audience does.

In the 1997 film *Titanic*, director James Cameron employs this perspective throughout his telling of the story. In an opening scene, Jack Dawson (Leonardo DiCaprio) wins a ticket for the maiden voyage of the great ship in a card game. We watch as Jack celebrates his good fortune. However, the audience cannot help but to watch through the lens of the story's end. We know that the ship will sink and, therefore, we cannot fully participate in Jack's excitement. Similarly, the known ending casts a shadow over the love story between Jack and Rose DeWitt Bukater (Kate Winslet). While we watch the two fall in love, we do this through the lens of the ship's impending destruction. In this case, our experience of the passion between the two is heightened because we know that it will also be short-lived.

The term "conclusion awareness" is one that I have invented. A formal term does not exist for the narrative technique that I have described. In other words, while James Cameron employed this tool in his storytelling, he did not use the term "conclusion awareness." The *term* is modern and unique to me. However, the *technique* is ancient and has been (and continues to be) widely used. Like other authors telling a story with a universally known ending, the author of the Gospel of Matthew used conclusion awareness. Again, I am not claiming that the gospel writer would have known or used this term. Rather, I am saying that the gospel is written with the assumption that while the characters do not yet know about the imminent death and resurrection of Jesus, the audience does. Furthermore, and most importantly, the audience views all of the events before the death and resurrection through the lens of the story's ending. Just as we cannot help but to imagine the torn ship when watching Jack and Rose, we cannot help but to imagine both the cross and the empty tomb when listening to Jesus. For some storytellers, this is a burden. Others employ conclusion awareness to great effect. The author of the Gospel of Matthew is just such a masterful storyteller.

The use of conclusion awareness is only possible when it can be assumed that the ending is universally known. When this is the case, the material that is included in the story is not only relevant to the outcome (it moves the story along), but is also meant to be interpreted through the lens of the story's ending. Perhaps it is helpful to consider an example from the Gospel of Matthew. We are told the story of a girl who has recently died. Her father, a leader of a synagogue, asks Jesus to lay his hands on her that she might live. When Jesus arrives at the home of the leader, he is met by flute players and a crowd that is making a great commotion. His announcement that the girl is not dead, but only sleeping, receives laughter. The story culminates in the resuscitation of the girl. Jesus takes her by the hand and she gets up (9:18–26). If the end of the gospel is unknown, the reader will likely laugh along with the crowd. Surely a girl who has died will stay dead. However, since the ending is known, the reader cannot help but to think about Jesus' own triumph over death, about the empty tomb and his resurrection. In this case, we are not surprised when the girl gets up. In fact, we expect this result. For readers, even readers new to this story, it is assumed that Jesus has power over the grave.

A universally known ending can be a burden. Imagine hearing a joke when you already know the punch line. Or, imagine being forced to sit through a story when you already know how it will end. The known ending becomes a burden for both the listener and the one telling the joke or story. In contrast, a universally known ending *can* be a powerful tool in the hands of a thoughtful storyteller. We ask, "How are you going to keep my attention? How are you going to tell this known story in an unknown way?" James Cameron's *Titanic* could have been a flop, a known story told again, without fresh insight. Instead, it was a box office hit. Cameron found a way to breathe life into what might have otherwise been a lifeless story. The Gospel of Matthew is a most powerful telling of the Jesus story. The author weaves the known ending, that *from expected death comes unexpected new life*, throughout the gospel. In the example above, we watch as Jesus brings a girl back to life. And in so doing, we experience the theme that from death comes life. Even though we know the ending, even though we know that Jesus has power over death, we are captivated. The theme is so well interwoven into the story that we can't wait to see how the theme will be used, how the story will be told.

Conclusion

The discussion of genre is a helpful and important way to begin our reading of the Gospel of Matthew. Just as an awareness of different film genres helps us to know what to expect from a movie, an awareness of the genre of ancient biography helps us to know what to expect from a gospel. In the case of the Gospel of Matthew, the goal of the author is twofold. First, the gospel is written to reveal the *character*, the *person*, of Jesus. Second, the gospel is not meant to be neutral, but is written to convince readers of the importance of Jesus. Furthermore, just as a movie might hold to a specific genre (romantic comedy, drama, etc.), but offer a distinct perspective or unique voice, our gospel weaves a distinct theme into the traditional biographical format. The gospel announces, again and again, with a poetic voice, that *from expected death comes unexpected new life.*

The most obvious example of the movement from death to life is that of Jesus' death and resurrection. While the story of the crucifixion and the empty tomb come at the end of the gospel, they are known from the very beginning. Some stories are like that. Some stories have endings that are so well known that they cast a shadow over every aspect, every element, of the narrative. When we read about the birth of Jesus, we are already thinking about the forthcoming crucifixion. When we listen to Jesus teach and preach, we are again thinking about how the story will end. The author uses this to great effect. We are invited to think about this movement from death to life every step along the way. We are invited to consider the theme *from expected death comes unexpected new life* throughout the entire gospel. And when we do, we experience in a new way the power and promise of the story of Jesus.

2
Great Beginnings

Unexpected New Life in Matthew's Genealogy

L et's face it: for a modern reader there isn't a worse way to begin the Gospel of Matthew than with a genealogy. Whether we are new to the gospel or already well acquainted with the story, it is tempting to skip the first seventeen verses (and perhaps also this chapter about them). And why not? Does knowing that Salathiel was the father of Zerubbabel help us to better understand the grand story that is to follow? If we are being completely honest, we are not even very good at knowing our own genealogies. If I were to provide you with unlimited paper and unlimited time, how far could you get with drawing your own family tree? I am guessing that outlining your immediate family would be relatively easy. But what happens when you jump back a generation or two? You may know first names. But, do you know middle names and birth dates? Most of us believe that history is important and we wish we knew more about our families. But, few of us take this enthusiasm to the next level and actually do the research. If we don't know our own personal histories, how much more unlikely is it that we will invest the time and energy necessary to understand the genealogy of Jesus?

To complicate matters, names are just names if they are not accompanied by stories. Testing this theory is easy. Share with someone the names of a few of your family members. At best, you will start a limited discussion concerning names. "You don't meet many people named 'Fred.'" But, if you share a story or two about each individual, the names are no longer just names; the names represent real people, people with interests and dreams and fears. Fred quickly becomes more than just the name of my father-in-law. After a few minutes, he is a person with his own interesting story. The same would be true for Zerubbabel (you remember, Salathiel's son). Unfortunately, many of the stories that would breathe life into Matthew's list of names have been lost. We are left with only names, names that seem to lie lifeless on the page.

So, what are our options? I suppose the most tempting option is to follow our instincts, to skip the first seventeen verses of Matthew and to move directly to the birth story of Jesus. But, if we do, we will miss the subtle, yet important, manner in which the author of Matthew integrates the theme *from expected death comes unexpected new life* into the long and rich story of Jesus. However, before we explore the role of this theme in Matthew's genealogy, it is helpful to outline briefly a few ways that the list of names is commonly read and interpreted.

"Jesus, the Son of David" (Or, the Importance of the Number 14)

The Gospel of Matthew begins, "An account of the genealogy of Jesus the Messiah, the son of David, the son of Abraham." This is followed by a list of names beginning with Abraham. This opening sentence is packed with meaning. In the first words of the gospel, the author is making the claim that in no uncertain terms Jesus is, indeed, the Messiah. The author is also drawing a direct line between Jesus and Israel's great king and leader, David.

The author tells us that it is fourteen generations from Abraham to King David. It is another fourteen generations from David to the deportation of the Israelites to Babylon. Finally, it is another fourteen generations from the Babylonian exile to the birth of Jesus, the Messiah (1:17). In Matthew's gospel, then, the genealogy of Jesus is neatly, evenly, and very purposefully divided into three sections of fourteen generations. Most English translations provide three paragraphs, each with fourteen generations. The reason for this organization is lost on us as twenty-first-century readers holding English translations of Matthew. Nevertheless, this structure was likely intentional. In Hebrew, each letter was associated with a number. The English equivalent would be to associate *A* with the number 1, *B* with 2, and so on. In this case, the name David, or *dvd* in Hebrew, was associated with the number 14. *D* (Dalet) is the fourth letter of the alphabet and *v* (Vav) is the sixth. The letters added together, *d* + *v* + *d*, or

4 + 6 + 4, total 14. By giving the genealogy of Jesus in three sections of 14 generations each, the author is emphasizing over and over and over again that Jesus is to be forever linked with David.

While the connection between Jesus and David may provide insight into the structure and purpose of Matthew's genealogy, it does not seem to introduce a central theme to the gospel. In fact, later in the gospel, Jesus himself questions the nature of the relationship between the Messiah and David. At the end of chapter 22, Jesus asks a group of Pharisees, "What do you think of the Messiah? Whose son is he?" The Pharisees answer Jesus, "The son of David." Jesus, however, challenges this seemingly correct answer. He asks the follow-up question, "How is it then that David by the Spirit calls him [the Messiah] Lord?" This question puts pressure on the Pharisees. Surely a father would not refer to his own son as "Lord." To be sure, there are many ways of interpreting this exchange between Jesus and the Pharisees. However, at the very least, this story makes it clear that the relationship between Jesus and David is not as easily understood as the genealogy seems to suggest. Moreover, while this relationship is emphasized (and the use of letters and numbers is very interesting), it does not prove to be a central theme that runs throughout the gospel.

"Jesus the Son of Adam, the Son of God"
(Or, Matthew and Luke Agree to Disagree)

While Jesus' genealogy in Matthew emphasizes, three times no less, that Jesus is the son of David, his genealogy in the Gospel of Luke is quite different. Even a casual comparison of the two lists reveals greater dissimilarity than similarity. This should not surprise those who have read both gospels. Luke and Matthew quite regularly present their narratives from different perspectives. The birth stories of Jesus prove to be an excellent example. Luke includes shepherds and angels and a manger. In Luke's gospel there is a census, with everyone traveling to their home cities to be registered. Matthew, in contrast, has a report of magi with three gifts and a great star. In Matthew, Herod kills all of the children in and around Bethlehem who are two years old or under. This massacre of infants is not reported by Luke.

The differences in the birth stories are undeniable. Yet, for many readers, they actually need to be pointed out. Why? The reason is simple: we are familiar with a harmonized version of the story. In December of every year, we are surrounded by nativity scenes that include shepherds and wise men, angels and a star. The two stories become one. Instead of reading each story and asking, "Why is the story told in this way?," we harmonize the stories and the unique perspective of each is lost. We do not ask, "Why does Luke emphasize shepherds?" Nor do we ask, "Why does Matthew emphasize the magi?" By combining the stories we think that we are covering over possible contradictions. But what we are really doing is losing the distinct voice of each gospel account.

Like the birth stories, the genealogies of Jesus in the Gospels of Matthew and Luke are different. Here, however, we do not bother to harmonize the two. Rather, we ignore them both. Luke, unlike Matthew, does not begin with Abraham, but rather describes Jesus as the "son of Adam, son of God." It is not, however, only the beginnings of the genealogies that are different. The lists of the generations leading up to Joseph bear little resemblance to one another. Again, the question we must ask is, "Why?" Does one gospel writer "get it wrong"? Or, should the genealogies be read less for their report of family history and more for their inclusion of an important idea or theme that runs throughout the gospel story? In other words, genealogies are best read as introductions to the person and story to follow rather than simple summaries of past events. Our questions, then, become, "Why does the Gospel of Matthew report Jesus' genealogy in this way? What does this genealogy tell us about the story of Jesus?"

Four Women and Mary

The genealogy of Jesus in Matthew's gospel is unique in that it includes four women and Mary. Why is this so significant? This lineage of Jesus was written in the first-century Mediterranean world, a culture based upon patrilineal descent. One's family was understood in terms of fathers and sons. Matthew's gospel is no exception. Every generation is described in terms of a father and a son; "Abraham was the father of Isaac, and Isaac was the father of Jacob," and so on down the line. However, at five points in this family history, a woman (the son's mother) is provided. Judah was the father of Perez and Zerah by Tamar (1:3). Salmon was the father of Boaz by Rahab (1:5). Boaz was the father of Obed by Ruth (1:5). David was the father of Solomon by the wife of Uriah (1:6). Finally, Joseph is the husband of Mary, who gave birth to Jesus (1:16).

For some readers, the very inclusion of women in the genealogy makes a point. Matthew, it may be argued, includes those that are regularly excluded. If you are looking for examples of radical inclusivity, there seems to be evidence in the very first verses of the gospel. However, such a reading raises more questions than it answers. Why does the author include only five women? Why not include other mother-son relationships? Moreover, why doesn't the author continue to emphasize women throughout the gospel? In the opening stories of Luke's gospel, for example, Mary and Elizabeth are given a voice while Joseph and Zechariah remain speechless. In contrast, the author of Matthew invites Joseph to speak in the birth account of Jesus, while Mary is silent. In short, the inclusion of five women in Matthew's genealogy of Jesus does not seem to introduce a special or emphasized role for women throughout the gospel story.

So, why does the author include *these* women? The most common answer to this question is that each woman was a Gentile (or non-Judean) and that each had some history of improper sexual activity. While this answer does provide some insight into the supposed shared experiences of the women, is this why the women were included? The author of Matthew does not seem to be concerned with the proper or improper sexual activity of women elsewhere in the gospel. For example, in the Gospel of John, Jesus encounters a Samaritan woman at a well. Even though the woman has been married five times and is currently living with a man that is not her husband, Jesus offers her living water (John 4:1–26). Later in John's gospel, a group of scribes and Pharisees brought to Jesus a woman who had been caught in adultery. They said to him, "Teacher, this woman was caught in the very act of committing adultery. Now in the law Moses commanded us to stone such women. Now what do you say?" After repeatedly questioning Jesus, he answered, "Let anyone among you who is without sin be the first to throw a stone at her." With this response, the men depart. Jesus announces to the woman that neither does he condemn her (John 8:1–11). Matthew's gospel does not include either story. In contrast, Jesus does explain, "You have heard that it was said, 'You shall not commit adultery.' But I say to you that everyone who looks at a woman with lust has already committed adultery with her in his heart" (Matthew 5:27–28). In short, Matthew does not integrate the type of discussions regarding adultery (or the proper and improper sexual activity of women) that we might expect based upon the supposed behavior of the women of the genealogy.

What if we are meant to draw meaning from something other than the sexual activity of the women in the genealogy of Jesus? If so, we are still left with the same set of questions. If the genealogy of Jesus is meant to introduce an idea or theme, rather than a rigid historical description of Jesus' family tree, what theme is being introduced? If the women included in the genealogy stand out as the unique feature of this list, why are they included? In short, what idea or theme is being introduced by these women?

The Women of Matthew's Genealogy as Agents of Unexpected New Life

Each of the women in Matthew's genealogy played a decisive role at a critical time in the Jesus family history. Put simply, each woman brought unexpected new life at a time when death was expected. While many readers emphasize the sexual activity of these women, this focus misses the broader and much more important issue: each woman was an agent of life during a time of expected death.

The story that dominates the last chapters of Genesis is that of Joseph (the one with the many-colored coat). The story of Joseph is so well known that it overshadows the stories of his brothers. Some would argue that this is just. After all, they were the ones that sold him into slavery. However, the genealogy of Jesus does not pass through Joseph, but rather through his half-brother, Judah. Therefore, it is Judah's story with which we are concerned.

The story of Judah picks up in Genesis 38 with the birth of his three sons: Er, Onan, and Shelah. When he is grown, the eldest son, Er, marries Tamar. Genesis reports that Er is wicked in the sight of the Lord and the Lord puts him to death. Next, Judah orders his second-born, Onan, to perform the duty of a brother-in-law and have offspring with Tamar. Onan, however, prevents the pregnancy from happening. This act is displeasing in the sight of the Lord and Onan is also put to death. At this point, Judah does not command his third-born son to go to Tamar. When Tamar discovers that Shelah has grown up, yet she has not been given to him in marriage, she dresses as a prostitute, tricks Judah, and becomes pregnant with Judah's son. This pregnancy insures that the line of Judah will continue.

The story is certainly not without plot twists. What wickedness does Er perform to warrant being killed by the Lord? Why do modern readers focus on the improper sexual activity of Tamar (pretending to be a prostitute) and neglect to mention the improper sexual activity of Onan, activity that warrants being killed by the Lord? Why doesn't Judah command his third-born, Shelah, to marry Tamar? In the end, only one thing is certain: it is the actions of Tamar that preserves the lineage of Judah. Without Tamar, the genealogy would end here. It is because of Tamar that from expected death comes unexpected new life.

Rahab is the second woman in Matthew's genealogy and, like Tamar, she proves to be an agent of unexpected new life. Our story picks up with Israel, a people, a nation, that has been promised a great land. After forty years of wilderness wandering under the leadership of Moses, Joshua is preparing to lead his people across the Jordan River and into the Promised Land. However, before this can happen, he sends two men to spy on the land and its inhabitants, especially the city of Jericho. The two men go there and enter the house of Rahab. Here we are told that Rahab is a prostitute. The king of Jericho finds out about the spies and confronts Rahab. If Rahab turns the men over to the king of Jericho, she will be thwarting the plans of the Israelites. This will mean the end to God's plan and the death of the promise. If Rahab conceals the spies and lies to the king of Jericho, she will allow for the plans of the Israelites, the plans of God, to continue. In so doing, Rahab provides life in a situation of expected death (Joshua 2:1–21; 6:22–25). It is interesting to note that it is only in Matthew's genealogy that Rahab is mentioned as Boaz's mother (or David's ancestor). This set of relationships is not mentioned in any other biblical passage.

Like that of Tamar, the story of Rahab is engaging. Readers are drawn into a great spy story. How did the king of Jericho find out about the men? Why are we told that Rahab is a prostitute? Moreover, why do so many modern readers emphasize this element of the story when she is not primarily remembered for her sexual activity in the writing of the New Testament? The author of Hebrews does note that Rahab was a prostitute, but she is celebrated for her faithfulness (11:31). Likewise, the author of James describes her as a prostitute, but remembers her for her good works and her role in insuring the continuation of God's plan (2:25). Again like the Tamar story, the importance of Rahab's actions is clear. It is Rahab that finds herself in a crucial position at a crucial time in Israel's history. The king of Jericho knows about the spies. The king of Jericho knows about the plans of the Israelites. The future of Israel is in the hands of this woman. Readers might expect the worst, to expect death. But Rahab is an agent of life, an agent of unexpected new life.

The book of Ruth is a short story with deep beauty and eloquence. It is a moving narrative that continues to capture the attention of every generation. And rightly so, this is a story of devotion and strength. It is the story of, Naomi, and her daughter-in-law, Ruth. The story begins with the death of Naomi's husband and both of her sons. She is alone. Without a family, she is without a future. So, Naomi decides to travel to the country of Moab where she has heard that the people have been blessed with food. She instructs both daughters-in-law to return to their families, that they might also find security, find a future. The women kiss one another and cry. Ruth, however, stays with Naomi. Their bond is strong and the two women face their futures together.

The women eventually meet a relative, Boaz, from the side of Naomi's late husband. We are told that Boaz is rich. The women begin their relationship with Boaz as workers in his field. As time passes, Naomi explains to Ruth that she must secure her future: she must have a child with Boaz. The story ends with the wedding of Boaz and Ruth and with a genealogy. It is this genealogy that reveals that King David is among their descendants (Ruth 2–4).

Where the stories of Tamar and Rahab were integrated into larger narratives, Tamar is a central figure in the story of Judah, and Rahab an essential character in the story of the exodus, Ruth receives her own book. There is no question that this story is Ruth's story. Her love and devotion to her mother-in-law, Naomi, is lifted up as a model for intimacy. Her trust that God will provide drives her every decision and action. To suggest that the story of Ruth can be understood in terms of her sexual activity alone is to neglect one of the great stories of the Bible. This is a story of death. The book begins with the death of Naomi's husband and two sons. The book suggests that without this family, the death of the women is imminent. Like Tamar and Rahab before her, Ruth occupies a crucial place in Israel's history. Without her faithfulness and action, she would not marry Boaz. Without this, there would be no descendants, no David. The story of Ruth makes clear that she is an agent of life, unexpected new life.

The fourth woman in Matthew's genealogy, the wife of Uriah, is not given a name. But the events, and her name, are well known. The story begins with David and his desire to be with Bathsheba. Bathsheba is married to Uriah, but this will not stop David from moving forward with his plan. David, the great king, orders Uriah, a soldier in his army, to move to the front of the battle lines. This order insures the death of Uriah and opens the way to an affair with Bathsheba. The actions of David do not, however, go unpunished. While Bathsheba becomes pregnant and bears a son, the Lord strikes the child with illness and it dies. Later, it is Bathsheba who gives birth to David's son, Solomon (2 Samuel 11–12).

Modern readers often emphasize the great beauty of Bathsheba, with whom David had his affair. The story itself, however, does not allow for Bathsheba to be pronounced guilty. David's closest friend, Nathan, condemns his behavior and it is the Lord that takes David's first son as punishment. The story of Bathsheba is again a story of death, both experienced and expected. Bathsheba experiences the death of her husband, Uriah. In addition, Bathsheba experiences the death of her firstborn. Importantly, the story does not end with death. Death and punishment do not have the final word. Bathsheba bears another son, Solomon, and our genealogy continues. It is "the wife of Uriah" that proves to be another agent of new life.

Conclusion

The genealogy of Matthew is unique. In three sections of fourteen generations, the lineage of Jesus moves from Abraham through Joseph and Mary. In addition, the list includes women, a surprising feature in its patriarchal context. But what does it mean? The names vary greatly from Luke's genealogy. Furthermore, neither the Gospels of Mark nor John even include a genealogy. So, why does Matthew? What is Matthew telling us in this list of mostly obscure names? Here, very powerfully, the author introduces a long history of unexpected new life rising from situations of expected death. God has worked though faithful women and men who have acted as agents of new life. With this the gospel begins. With this we are introduced to Jesus, the ultimate agent of new life.

3
Joseph's Dilemma

Unexpected New Life in the Birth Story of Jesus

For most of us, the story of the birth of Jesus brings to mind Christmas hymns, trees, gifts, and celebrations. This is a story, we assume, of a simple and beautiful event. It is the very human and humble beginning of what will be the great life of Jesus. We might not immediately relate to stories of lepers. We might have a hard time imagining the transfiguration. But the birth of Jesus? Surely this is a story to which we can all relate. We can imagine the joy of both Mary and Joseph as they hold their newborn son for the first time. We can hear Jesus' first attempts at crying. The birth of a child is both scary and wonderful. Babies are so fragile and yet so full of promise. After the genealogy, this is the first story in our gospel. Is there a better way to set the scene? Is there a better way to introduce us to the life of Jesus? What might come as a surprise is that this is also the first story to introduce the theme that from expected death comes unexpected new life.

The story is only eight verses long, but at the center of the account is Joseph's dilemma (1:18–25). We are told, "When Mary had been engaged to Joseph, but before they lived together, she was found to be with child from the Holy Spirit." While Joseph discovers that Mary is pregnant, he does not know that she is with child from the Holy Spirit. This is made known to Joseph later by an angel who appears to him in a dream. In the mean time, Joseph must decide what he will do with Mary. In other words, the story does not actually focus on the birth of Jesus. At the heart of the story is Joseph's dilemma. What should he do when confronted with the pregnancy of Mary?

We are told that Joseph is a righteous man and is unwilling to expose Mary to public disgrace. So, he plans to "dismiss her quietly." But what does it mean to "dismiss her quietly"? Most of us envision one option—that of divorce. The dilemma, we assume, is whether Joseph should divorce Mary publicly or privately. While we assume that Joseph is contemplating divorce, this assumption represents *our* cultural experience rather than the cultural reality of the first-century Mediterranean world. In sharp contrast to divorce, Joseph's dilemma involves an assumption of adultery and the subsequent possibility of the killing of Mary. Worded differently, Joseph's dilemma involves the possibility of an honor killing. If Joseph reveals that Mary is pregnant, she will be killed. If Joseph conceals Mary's pregnancy, he will be opposing the law of the Lord. What is a righteous man to do?

For some of us, this may be difficult to accept. In fact, it may sound offensive that the birth story and Joseph's dilemma involves the possible murder of Mary (and, therefore, the killing of Jesus). This reading, however, not only reflects the cultural reality of the Bible, it actually builds upon the important theme that from expected death comes unexpected new life.

A Culture of Honor and Shame

The study of the ancient Mediterranean world and its culture has helped us better understand the words and deeds of the people of the Bible. However, while we might be aware that our modern American culture differs greatly from the culture of the Gospel of Matthew, it is still very hard for us not to read the gospel from our cultural perspective. We may consider what *we* would do if *we* were dealing with an unexpected pregnancy, but what would *Joseph* be thinking? What would *Joseph* be feeling?

Our reading of the birth of Jesus must begin with a discussion of the Mediterranean cultural values of honor and shame. It is honor that is most valued. But more than that, it is honor that defines a person. Your honor represents your value, where you stand in society. Because of this, honor is socially determined. It is not determined by oneself, but has to be recognized by others. In other words, it is the community that determines how much honor one has. And, it is in comparison with others in the community that defines your social worth. Do you have more or less honor? We witness this throughout the Gospel of Matthew. Shepherds and children have little social value, little honor. Those with skin diseases and those who are blind have little social value or honor. But how is one's honor actually determined?

There are two ways in which individuals receive honor. First, honor is *ascribed*. This is the honor status that you receive at birth. For example, you receive the honor status of your family and of your town. Are you born into a family with little honor, or great honor? How do others estimate the honor of your hometown? This is, of course, out of your control. Some people are born with much honor; others are not. However, honor can also be *acquired*. You can challenge the honor of others through a wide variety of interactions. Through public challenges and responses, honor is either protected or lost. All the while, this is a social activity. In other words, it is up to the community to determine the winner and the loser in an honor challenge.

When reading the birth story of Jesus, the consideration of ascribed honor is interesting. What kind of honor is Jesus born with? How do people view Nazareth? While this is interesting, our reading of the birth story, and our understanding of honor killings, depends upon our awareness of acquired honor. Many of the social interactions in the Gospel of Matthew are competitions, or challenges, for honor. Even the smallest of actions can be a challenge to one's honor. For example, asking a question in public is often an honor challenge. Does the one addressed know the answer? Do they fumble for the answer? Did the answer come so quickly and easily that the one asking the question now looks shamed? How do others view the exchange? These interactions take the form of a challenge and response. While most challenges are verbal, they can also be physical or in the form of a gesture or a look. In every case, the interplay between challenge and response is a social contest. After exchanges are made, spectators determine the winner. There is evidence of these challenges on nearly every page of our gospel. When the Pharisees ask Jesus a question, it is often much more than a question it is an honor challenge.

Finally, we must understand the role of family honor. It is family honor that is emphasized over individual honor. To be more exact, one's honor is dependent on the honor of the family. Honor challenges, then, are not simply between two people, they are challenges to the very families in which the individuals belong. Losing an honor challenge may bring shame upon the entire family. And, when a family member is challenged, the entire family often acts. After all, the honor of the whole family is at stake. In the case of an honor killing, it is the honor of the entire family that is threatened when a female member is believed to have engaged in improper sexual behavior. Worded differently, if the actions of a sister or daughter are thought to be shameful, the honor of the entire family is at stake. And, the family has to respond to the challenge.

The Modern Practice of Honor Killings

If the males in a family feel that they must respond to a loss of honor due to the sexual activity of a female family member, what are their options? Or, what is an honor killing? Simply stated, an honor killing is the practice of killing a girl or woman who is thought to have endangered her family's honor by engaging in inappropriate sexual activity. While many (perhaps most) examples of honor killings occur when a girl loses her virginity before marriage, this is not the only sexual activity that is punished by death. Honor killings are also executed in some instances of rape, child sexual abuse, and even flirting. Moreover, the mere allegation of improper behavior on the part of a girl or woman may be enough to defile a family's honor and "warrant" an honor killing.

While such killings occur at an alarming rate, where are they actually taking place? The majority of honor killings occur in the Middle East. However, the practice of honor killing is widespread. Honor killings have been reported in Afghanistan, Bangladesh, China, Egypt, Ecuador, India, Iran, Iraq, Israel, Italy, Jordan, Korea, Lebanon, Pakistan, Palestine, Morocco, Sweden, Syria, Turkey, Uganda, Yemen, the United Kingdom, and the United States. Furthermore, the murder of women over family honor occurs in Latin America. There, the term that is used is "crime of passion." In short, honor killings occur in any cultural context that is highly patriarchal and that places great emphasis on family honor.

How often do honor killings occur? To be sure, it is impossible to know the actual number of girls and women killed each year. One reason that it is difficult to assess the frequency of honor killings is that the practice often remains a private family affair with no official statistics or records made available. However, the United Nations estimates that more than five thousand women worldwide are killed each year in the name of family honor. Behind this staggering statistic is the reality that there is often an absence of a proper law to punish the perpetrators. For example, if an Iraqi male is found guilty of committing an honor killing today, the maximum sentence is one year in prison.

Descriptions of Honor Killings in Narrative Form

Evidence of the practice of honor killings is found in a wide variety of places. Poetry is written by women describing the violence. Documentaries have been made that expose the reality. While newspapers provide the facts, it is often in alternative sources that the practice is more vividly described. In other words, it is often through very personal stories that families share their experiences with this violent crime. The most accessible example is a 2005 biography written by a woman named Souad. As a girl, Souad was a resident of a small village in the West Bank. She describes her experience of surviving an attempted honor killing in her book, *Burned Alive*.

Souad had an affair with a young man before marriage. She loved the boy and believed that they would be together. However, he abandoned her shortly after she became pregnant. When her pregnancy was discovered by her family, it was decided that she must be killed. She explains that if a girl dishonors her family, everyone in the village rejects the family. They do not speak to them or do business with them. Because of her actions, her family felt forced to defend its honor and to restore its public standing. As Souad worked in the yard, gasoline was poured over her head and she was set on fire. Remarkably, Souad survived the attempted honor killing. During her time in the hospital, she defended the actions of her family and her mother. She felt that her mother was doing her duty to sentence her to death. She even felt guilty that it was taking her so long to die, for this was only extending the family's shame.

While Souad survived the attempted murder, she was forced to endure great suffering in her long battle back to health. Finally, she moved to Europe, where she now lives with her husband (not the young man with whom she had the affair) and their three children. Remarkably, her telling of her story concludes with her being reunited with the child of her pregnancy, a son, with whom she was burned years before.

Honor Killings: Religious or Cultural Practice?

For many, an essential question remains when considering the practice of honor killings: Are honor killings a religious or a cultural practice? Worded differently, and much more frankly, are honor killings a Muslim practice? There is a tendency among many Americans to view the practice of honor killings as a "Muslim issue." This view is incorrect. Honor killings are practiced by Hindus, Sikhs, Christians, Jews, and Muslims. It is necessary to emphasize that Arab Christians, who are a minority in the Middle East, do commit honor killings. However, it is also necessary to emphasize that while honor killings do occur in both Muslim and Christian communities, the practice is not dictated by the religious doctrine of *either* group. In other words, honor killings do not occur because of Muslim or Christian beliefs. Rather, honor killings occur in patriarchal cultures that place a high value on family honor.

Some people are surprised that this practice even occurs. Furthermore, some doubt that it occurs in a modern Christian context. In 2005, one particular honor killing received significant attention in the British media. This may be due to the fact that it occurred within a Palestinian Christian family. A Christian father from Palestine killed his daughter in their home after discovering that she intended to marry a Muslim. For the father, such a marriage was assumed to be shameful. The family's honor was at stake. The father, Faten Habash, promised an emissary from a Bedouin tribe, traditionally brought in to mediate matters of family honor, that he would not kill his daughter. However, as the twenty-two-year-old woman watched a Boy Scout parade from the balcony of their Ramallah home, her father dragged her into the living room and bludgeoned her with an iron bar.

In this case, the act of marrying a Muslim was understood to be a threat to the family's honor. However, in most cases, it is the sexual activity (or presumed sexual activity) of a girl that is understood to be the threat. It is impossible to overstate the importance of a woman's virginity throughout the patriarchal societies of the Middle East and the Mediterranean world. A woman's virginity is the "property" of the men around her. Before she is married, it represents the honor of her father and the family. Upon marriage, a woman's virginity is a gift for her husband. Her sexual purity is now the property of her new family. If she is not a virgin on the wedding night, the marriage begins with an unforgivable shame.

Because the virginity of women is a symbol of family honor, it is fiercely guarded by the males in the family. In other words, if a girl brings shame upon the family by her loss of virginity, the honor of the whole family is at risk. Men, then, feel that they must protect the virginity of their sisters and daughters at all costs. We witness the preoccupation that Mediterranean males have with the virginity of women in their use of language. In the Arabic vocabulary, the word for "virgin" refers to women only, never men. There is not a masculine equivalent. In fact, if you wish to refer to men who have had no sexual experience before marriage, there is not a convenient term to use.

A Warning against Making This All about "Them"

Instructors of Middle East Studies emphasize a tendency among many Americans. Whether intentional or not, the discussion of honor killings can quickly become a discussion of "us" and "them," with "their" actions described in particularly negative terms. We ask, "Can you believe that in some parts of the world men treat their wives and daughters with such violence?" An examination of honor killings often has the effect of perpetuating the stereotype that Middle Eastern societies are uniquely violent toward women. We must fight against this tendency.

There are various ways to fight against such an us-versus-them reading. Anthropologists always discuss the issue of honor killings in terms of human rights. In other words, honor killings must be understood as one way, among many, that men control and oppress women throughout the world. Perhaps the issue of honor killing does not seem to impact our cultural situation immediately, but violence against women surely does. An examination of rape, incest, and other sexual violence in our country proves to be shocking and embarrassing. In other words, we cannot look upon what "they" do without also considering what "we" do. In every culture, in every country, women experience terrible violence at the hands of men—often times, at the hands of the very men who profess to love them. Everyone, then, is forced to consider the oppression of women present in their own society. Another strategy to fight against an us-versus-them reading is to consider the many examples of resistance. While honor killings do continue to occur at alarming rates, public resistance to the crime is growing. For example, the Palestinian feminist organization al-Fanar organizes marches against honor killings. In other words, even in the patriarchal cultures that emphasize family honor, not all members understand honor killings to be acceptable or appropriate.

Joseph's *Awareness of* and *Reaction to* Mary's Pregnancy

So, what does this all mean for our reading of the birth story in the Gospel of Matthew? We are, after all, considering the birth of Jesus, not examining a modern practice of violence. Our understanding of Joseph's dilemma begins with his becoming aware of Mary's pregnancy. What did Joseph believe about the pregnancy? Quite simply, the story itself requires us to come to the conclusion that Joseph assumed that Mary had committed adultery. We, as the readers, are provided with information that is not known to Joseph. Mary is with child—through the Holy Spirit. We are told this information, but Joseph is not; at least not until the end of the story. While we do not face a dilemma, it is clear from the story that Joseph does. The dilemma continues until an angel of the Lord appears to Joseph in a dream. Since the story itself makes real the dilemma faced by Joseph, we too must closely consider his dilemma.

Joseph's dilemma is based upon one central question: if he suspects Mary of adultery, what are his options? As modern readers, we are nearly unanimous in the belief that divorce is the only *real* option. In fact, we typically do not even discuss or consider other options. For us, the question is whether or not Joseph ought to make his divorce of Mary public or private. In turn, we believe that a public divorce would bring shame upon Mary and a private divorce would minimize her disgrace. In short, we do not understand the dynamics of family honor. It is not Mary's honor (in our understanding of the term) that is at stake. Rather, it is the honor of her family. If Mary has committed adultery, the honor of her family has been threatened. Subsequently, her family must defend its honor. So, Joseph is faced with a dilemma. Does he reveal the pregnancy? If he does, her pregnancy will threaten the honor of her family, and they will likely attempt to defend their honor by killing Mary. If he does not, he is hiding the pregnancy, hiding the adultery, and going against the law of the Lord.

Honor Killing in Ancient Jewish Literature

Did such violence actually occur in the ancient Mediterranean world? It is ironic that we are able to imagine Herod killing children, Rome persecuting early Christians, and even imagine the act of crucifixion, but we may not be willing to concede that brothers and fathers killed their sisters and daughters when family honor was at stake. Therefore, it is helpful for us to consider a number of examples of honor killings (or the threat of honor killings) from the Old Testament and ancient Jewish literature.

In the book of Susanna (in the Apocrypha), a rich man, Joakim, is married to the very beautiful Susanna. Joakim's house has a large garden and the Judeans often visit his house because he is honorable. Among the visitors are two elders who have been appointed as judges. They are frequently at Joakim's house and all who have a case to be tried come to them there. As time passes, both elders begin to lust for Susanna. Day after day, they wait eagerly to see her. On one particularly hot day, Susanna decides to bathe outdoors, in the garden. The elders wait and watch as Susanna is left alone and the garden doors are closed. Once they are alone with Susanna, the elders make their presence and their lustful intentions known.

With their actions, Susanna is presented with a dilemma. She will either be raped by the elders or be falsely accused of adultery. In either case, she will be killed. Since she is faced with a death sentence either way, she refuses the men and plans to die because of the false accusations of the elders. At least that way she will not actually commit the sin of adultery in the sight of the Lord.

> When the maids had gone out, the two elders got up and ran to her. They said, "Look, the garden doors are shut, and no one can see us. We are burning with desire for you; so give your consent, and lie with us. If you refuse, we will testify against you that a young man was with you, and this was why you sent your maids away." Susanna groaned and said, "I am completely trapped. For if I do this, it will mean death for me; if I do not, I cannot escape your hands. I choose not to do it; I will fall into your hands, rather than sin in the sight of the Lord. "(vv. 19–22)

The next day, as people gather at the house of Joakim, the elders come, plotting to have Susanna put to death. As the people listen, the elders falsely accuse Susanna of adultery.

> "While we were walking in the garden alone, this woman came in with two maids, shut the garden doors, and dismissed the maids. Then a young man, who was hiding there, came to her and lay with her. We were in a corner of the garden, and when we saw this wickedness we ran to them. Although we saw them embracing,

we could not hold the man, because he was stronger than we are, and he opened the doors and got away. We did, however, seize this woman and asked who the young man was, but she would not tell us. These things we testify." (36–41)

After hearing the accusation, the assembly of Judeans accepts the false testimony of the elders and condemns Susanna to death. It is important to note that this story does not describe a formal trial, but rather emphasizes the community's role in determining the winner and loser in the honor challenge. In this case, the community determines that Susanna's actions have brought shame to the house of Joakim. In response, Susanna must be killed.

The story concludes with Susanna's innocence and life restored. She cries out to the Lord and the wickedness and lies of the elders are exposed. However, the story reveals an important dynamic of ancient Judean culture: the elders, Susanna (and presumably Joakim), and the Judean assembly all assume that if Susanna has committed adultery she will be killed. In addition, this story also reveals that an honor killing may occur even if there is no "proof" of adultery. In this case a false accusation is enough to sentence a woman to death.

Another example of the assumption that death is the appropriate penalty for adultery is found in the writing of the first-century Jewish historian, Josephus. In his description of the adultery of David with Bathsheba, he notes that when Bathsheba became pregnant her sin had to be concealed; for, according to the laws of the fathers, she was deserving of death as an adulteress (*Jewish Antiquities* 7.131). Similarly, the relationship between adultery and family honor is a reoccurring theme in the writing of the Jewish philosopher Philo. According to him, adultery is the greatest of all crimes. While he provides several reasons to justify this claim, he emphasizes the damage done to family honor.

Indeed it makes havoc of three families; of that of the husband who suffers from the breach of faith, stripped of the promise of his marriage-vows and his hopes of legitimate offspring, and of two others, those of the adulterer and the woman, for the infection of the outrage and dishonour and disgrace of the deepest kind extends to the family of both. (*On the Decalogue* 126)

Philo does not stop with a discussion of the damage done to family honor through adultery; he repeatedly explains that the proper punishment for adultery is death. In describing a woman suspected of adultery, he notes that she is threatened by two dangers. First, she is in danger of losing her life. Second, she is in danger of bringing shame on her past. He notes that the latter danger is a far more grievous thing than death (*On the Special Laws* 3.52–54). Time and time again, we see that the discussion of death as the appropriate punishment for adultery is ancient.

Adultery and Honor Killing in the Gospel of John

The assumption that death is the appropriate punishment for adultery is also present in the New Testament. John 8:1–11 is the story of a woman who has been caught in adultery. In the story, Jesus is sitting and teaching at the temple in Jerusalem. A number of scribes and Pharisees bring the woman and place her in the midst of the group that is gathered around Jesus. They ask, "Teacher, this woman was caught in the very act of committing adultery. Now the law Moses commanded to us to stone such women. Now what do you say?" (8:4–5). This story includes a *double* honor challenge. First, the scribes and Pharisees challenge the honor of Jesus by asking him to interpret the Law of Moses. Second, adultery is understood to be a challenge, or threat, to family honor. Will Jesus defend his honor by answering the question, by answering the challenge? Will Jesus uphold the ancient assumptions of honor and shame, of chastity and death, and sentence this woman to be stoned?

The scribes and Pharisees continue to question Jesus. After a time, Jesus says to the group, "Let anyone among you who is without sin be the first to throw a stone at her" (8:7). After this response, the group goes away one by one, beginning with the elders. When Jesus is left alone with the woman, he asks, "Woman, where are they? Has no one condemned you?" (8:10). The woman replies, "No one, sir." He then proclaims, "Neither do I condemn you. Go your way, and from now on do not sin again" (8:11).

In this story, Jesus responds to both challenges. First, he defends his honor through a response in the form of a corresponding challenge to the scribes and Pharisees. It is they, not he, who are shamed, for not one is found to be free from sin. Second, Jesus responds to the ancient assumptions of adultery and death. While Jesus does acknowledge the sin, he challenges the assumption that such an act should be punishable by death. Important for us is the assumption held by the scribes and Pharisees (and presumably by the group gathered around Jesus) that adultery is, and ought to be, punishable by death.

Early Christian Interpretation of the Birth Story in Matthew

How did early Christians understand Joseph's dilemma? Did they assume that it involved the decision between public or private divorce? Or, did early Christians assume that Joseph's dilemma included the very real possibility that Mary might be killed? *The Infancy Gospel of James* provides insight into how early Christians interpreted the story of the birth of Jesus. This non-canonical gospel was written in the later half of the second century and was very popular for hundreds of years.

The *Infancy Gospel of James* tells the story of two important births. It begins with the birth of Mary, and tells of her childhood and her engagement to Joseph. The gospel also tells the story of the birth of Jesus and extends through Herod's killing of the infants. Most important for us is that the text builds upon the Gospel of Matthew by providing a more detailed picture of the birth of Jesus. The additional material reveals that Joseph's dilemma is not that of public versus private divorce, but was indeed that of the possible honor killing of Mary. Joseph reasons that if he does not reveal Mary's pregnancy, he will be going against the law of the Lord. However, if he does reveal Mary's pregnancy, he will be handing her over to a death sentence.

> [13:1]She was in her sixth month when one day Joseph came home from his building projects, entered his house, and found her pregnant. [2]He struck himself in the face, threw himself to the ground on sackcloth, and began to cry bitterly; "What sort of face should I present to the Lord God? [3]What prayer can I say on her behalf since I received her as a virgin from the temple of the Lord God and didn't protect her? [4]Who has set this trap for me? Who has done this evil deed in my house? Who has lured this virgin away from me and violated her? [5]The story of Adam has been repeated in my case hasn't it? For just as Adam was praying when the serpent came and found Eve alone, deceived her, and corrupted her, so the same thing has happened to me." [6]So Joseph got up from the sackcloth and summoned Mary and said to her, "God has taken a special interest in you – how could you have done this? [7]Have you forgotten the Lord your God? Why have you brought shame on yourself, you who were raised in the Holy of Holies and fed by a heavenly messenger?" [8]But she began to cry bitter tears: "I'm innocent. I haven't

had sex with any man." [9]And Joseph said to her, "Then where did the child you're carrying come from?" [10]And she replied, "As the Lord my God lives, I don't know where it came from."

[14:1]And Joseph became very frightened and no longer spoke with her as he pondered what he was going to do with her. [2]And Joseph said to himself, "If I try to cover up her sin, I'll end up going against the law of the Lord. ([3]And if I disclose her condition to the people of Israel, I'm afraid that the child inside her might be heaven-sent and I'll end up handing innocent blood over to a death sentence. [4]So what should I do with her? [I know,] I'll divorce her quietly." [5]But when night came a messenger of the Lord suddenly appeared to him in a dream and said: "Don't be afraid of this girl, because the child in her is the holy spirit's doing. [6]She will have a son and you will name him Jesus – the name means 'he will save his people from their sins.'" [7]And Joseph got up from his sleep and praised the God of Israel, who had given him this favor [8]And so he began to protect the girl.

The author reveals two important assumptions regarding Joseph's dilemma. First, Joseph assumes that Mary has committed adultery. Second, Joseph assumes that if Mary's adultery and subsequent pregnancy is made known, she will be killed. In other words, this story describes with clarity and certainty that early Christians understood Joseph's dilemma to be that of the possible honor killing of Mary.

Another example of Joseph's dilemma being that of an honor killing comes from an early Christian interpretation of the birth story of Jesus in the Gospel of Matthew. While little is known regarding the historical context of this work, the anonymous author does make clear that Joseph's dilemma is that of the honor killing of Mary.

> Perhaps Joseph thought within himself: If I should conceal her sin, I would be acting against God's law, and if I should publicize it to the sons of Israel, they would stone her. I fear that what is in her womb is of divine intervention. Didn't Sarah conceive when she was ninety years of age and bring forth a child? If God caused that woman who was like dry wood to flower, what if the Godhead wanted Mary to bear a child without the aid of a man? . . . What shall I do then? I will put her away secretly, because it is better in an uncertain matter that a known prostitute should get off free than that an innocent person should die. It is indeed more just that an unjust person should escape justly than that a just person should die unjustly. If a guilty person should escape once, he can

die another time. But if an innocent person should die once, he
cannot be brought back. (*Patriologiae Cursus Completus* 56:633)

This account differs from the *Infancy Gospel of James* in Joseph's consideration of the origin of Mary's pregnancy. Here, Joseph wonders whether
it is God who is the cause of Mary's pregnancy. Ironically, the pregnancy
is still described as a sin. Importantly, even though the author does not
portray Joseph as suspecting Mary of adultery, his dilemma remains the
same. Should Joseph reveal Mary's sin? Or, should Joseph publicize her
sin to the sons of Israel? If her pregnancy is discovered, she will be the
victim of an honor killing.

Conclusion: What Is a Righteous Man to Do?

We return to the story of the birth of Jesus in the Gospel of Matthew. The
focus of the story is not on when. We are not told the day or date or year.
The focus on the story is not on where. We are not told anything about the
location. In fact, very little emphasis is placed on the birth itself. Rather, at
the heart of the story is Joseph's dilemma. Mary is pregnant. Furthermore,
Joseph assumes that she has committed adultery. So, what is he to do?
Should he reveal or conceal Mary's pregnancy? If it is revealed, she will be
killed. If it is concealed, he is going against the law of the Lord. So, what
is a righteous man to do?

Fortunately, we do not have to wait for Joseph's decision. Before he
is forced to decide, an angel of the Lord appears to him. Joseph is told
that the child is from the Holy Spirit and that when the child is born, he
is to name him Jesus. Just as we felt the agony of Joseph's dilemma, we
are now relieved. We expected death. But, Mary will not be killed, and
the child inside of her will be born. In the Gospel of Matthew, the birth
story of Jesus, the story of Joseph's dilemma, builds upon the theme
that was introduced in the genealogy: from expected death comes unexpected new life.

4

The Call to Discipleship as a Matter of Death and New Life

It seems that the author of our gospel could not have given less information regarding the call of Jesus' disciples if he had tried. Listen again to the call story of Matthew.

> As Jesus walked along, he saw a man called Matthew sitting at the tax booth; and he said to him, "Follow me." And he got up and followed him. (9:9)

That's it . . . one verse. As modern readers, we want more. We want to know answers to the questions of who, what, where, and when. Who was this Matthew? It is safe to say that he was a tax collector. But we want to know more. How old was he? Was he married? What was he like as a person? What is the context of this story? Was Jesus specifically looking for disciples? Did he have the number twelve in mind when he started? Where did this happen? Surely this information would have been easy enough to provide. We are told that Jesus was "walking along." Fine, but this is hardly helpful when we are trying to imagine the life of Jesus and his first conversations with his disciples. Was he walking along the beach? Walking along a busy street? Was it morning, evening; when did it occur?

If we are not provided with any of the traditional historical information (who, what, where, when), we are certainly not provided with an answer to the more interesting question of why. Why did Jesus call Matthew? Did Jesus see something in this man that was special? Why did Matthew drop everything and follow Jesus? What made Jesus' invitation

so appealing? Had Matthew heard of Jesus? Try to imagine the conver-
sation that immediately followed this event. "So, you say your name is
Jesus? It's nice to meet you. Where are we headed?"

There are only two call narratives in the entire gospel: the call of
Matthew (which we just reviewed) and the call of four fishermen, two
sets of brothers.

> As he walked by the Sea of Galilee, he saw two brothers, Simon,
> who is called Peter, and Andrew his brother, casting a net into the
> sea—for they were fishermen. And he said to them, "Follow me,
> and I will make you fish for people." Immediately they left their
> nets and followed him. As he went from there, he saw two other
> brothers, James son of Zebedee and his brother John, in the boat
> with their father Zebedee, mending their nets, and he called them.
> Immediately they left the boat and their father, and followed him.
> (4:18–22)

This story is longer than that of the call of Matthew, but does it provide us
with any additional information? In Matthew's story we learned his name
(Matthew), what he was doing (sitting at the tax booth), we heard Jesus'
invitation ("Follow me"), and we witnessed Matthew's response (he gets
up and follows Jesus). The same is true for the story above. We learn the
names of the two sets of brothers (Simon/Peter and Andrew; James and
John), we hear what they are doing (casting a net; fixing their nets), we
hear Jesus' invitation to Simon and Andrew ("Follow me, and I will make
you fish for people"), and we witness their responses (they follow him).

Again, that's it. Jesus will entrust so much to this group of followers,
and yet we are told so little about them. Perhaps it is this lack of historical
data that encourages us to jump, almost immediately, to the context of
our own lives. We read the stories of the call of the disciples and we ask,
"What would I have done?" Our questions are important and seemingly
endless. Does Jesus continue to call us today? To what task am I being
called? It doesn't take long for us to jump from the stories in Matthew to
the story of our own life. And, this is good. The stories in Matthew's gospel must (and do) continue to speak to every new generation of readers.
But, perhaps there is more to these stories than meets the eye? Perhaps
asking different questions, we will be surprised by the depth, the richness
of each story?

We will, in fact, find that the call of the disciples means a death—an
end to their lives as they know it. Their call is also a new beginning, the

beginning of an unexpected life that comes by following Jesus. Next, we will ask, "What can the disciples expect if they following Jesus?" Here we will learn that the disciples can expect persecution and death. They can also expect a promised new life, a life of salvation. Finally, the crucifixion and death of Jesus and the resurrection and new life of Jesus is mirrored by the experiences of the disciples. As Jesus experiences death, the disciples betray and deny him. As Jesus experiences new life, the disciples affirm their call and are sent into the world to spread the message of unexpected new life.

"Follow Me": The Call of the Disciples

A dominant value in modern American culture is individualism. It seems that every study of American culture begins here, and rightly so. From birth, we have been raised to see ourselves as unique and independent. Even though we may be members of groups (families, schools, teams, congregations, community groups), as Americans we prefer a loosely knit social framework. In other words, we want to be free to come and go, to join and quit, and to pick and choose group memberships that meet *our* needs. We feel free to move, make new friends, change schools, switch jobs, and even change spouses and families if we feel that our needs are not being met. In short, it is the individual that is most important and it is our individual needs that often take priority.

We also believe that every individual has a right to a private life and personal opinions. We yearn for private time and personal space. Many children are provided with their own bedroom where they are free to keep their personal belongings and to experience alone time. Closely related to the issue of privacy is our emphasis upon personal choice. Parents provide infants with choices before they are even able to choose. We ask, "Do you want apple sauce or peaches? Do you want to wear the pink or the yellow dress?" For the rest of our lives we are confronted with choices. And behind each choice lies the assumption that we are all unique individuals with our own opinions, interests, and needs.

Notice that the questions that come most naturally to us regarding the disciples are questions based upon our sense of individualism. We want to know what the disciples were like as individuals. What were their thoughts, their strengths, their weaknesses? When the gospel does not provide such information, we believe that the stories are lacking in necessary details.

It must be said that most of us do, of course, feel strong commitments to many of the groups to which we belong. We are faithful to our families; we are loyal to a variety of clubs and organizations. While this is true, our tendency toward individualism is still much stronger than most of the world's population. In fact, individualists are not the majority of people in the world today. And, they were certainly not present in the ancient Mediterranean world. Harry C. Triandis, professor emeritus in the Department of Psychology at the University of Illinois at Urbana-Champaign, estimates that 30 percent of the world are individualists while 70 percent are collectivists. He notes that Central and South America, Asia, Africa, and Arab-speaking countries tend to be collectivist, while individualism tends to be found in the USA, the nations of Northern and Western Europe, and Australia and New Zealand. Furthermore, individualism as we know it did not even exist anywhere in the Mediterranean world of the first century. Culturally speaking, the world of Matthew's gospel was a world of collectivism.

So, what is collectivism? People in collectivist cultures put a high value on conformity. Rather than seeing themselves as unique individuals, the collectivist strives to adhere to the accepted norms and behaviors of the group. Collectivist cultures tend to be organized hierarchically, with superiors making decisions for the group. In most collectivist cultures, the dominant group is the extended family, and family members feel interdependent and display a great deal of loyalty and solidarity to the group. Group members share resources and are primarily concerned with the success of the collective. Perhaps most importantly, one's self identity is defined in terms of the group identity. Where we might reason, "To know me is to know how I am unique, special, and how I stand out from the group," the collectivist believes, "I am known by the group of which I am a member. To know the group is to know me." Remember, the men and women who populate the New Testament were collectivist in nature. That means that the disciples held very different perceptions of identity than we do as twenty-first-century Americans.

For the disciples, the call to follow Jesus meant to break from their family, to leave all that they had known, to leave their social network, to forfeit the security that came with being a member of the group. In fact, to leave their families and to follow Jesus meant to replace their past identity with a new identity. This was a radical move. To us, the call stories seem to be lacking essential information. Jesus says, "Follow me," and the disciples follow him. We ask, "Is that all?" But, that is not all. An ancient audience would naturally have read between the lines, gathering a great deal from these simple narratives. The disciples leave all that they have, all that they have known. This is the death of their previous identities. We are told that the sons of Zebedee left the boat *and their father*. This is a very telling detail. The disciples, as they *were*, are dead. What lies ahead for them is unknown, unexpected, and new. The call stories of the disciples, then, are stories of death. The world that was known by the disciples has ended. But, the call to follow Jesus also signals unexpected new life—a new identity and a new future.

What Can Be Expected?: The Life of Discipleship

So, what can the disciples expect? As the disciples experience the death of their old selves and look forward to the unexpected life that comes with a new identity in Jesus, what does this mean for them? The entire tenth chapter of Matthew outlines the mission of the Twelve and the new life that is theirs to experience. Stated simply, this is a life of persecution, hatred, and death.

Jesus warns the disciples of the persecution that awaits them. The warning is extensive and graphic. The disciples are being sent out like sheep into the midst of wolves (10:16). They will be handed over to councils and will be flogged (10:17). They will be dragged before governors and kings (10:18). During this time of trial, brothers will betray brothers to death. A father will betray his child. Children will rise against parents and have them put to death (10:21). Finally, they will be hated by everyone (10:22). Not only is Jesus graphic in his description of coming events, he also provides an answer to the question, "Whom shall the disciples fear?" Apparently, they are not to fear those that persecute, for they can only destroy the body. Fear is to be reserved for the one that can destroy both body and soul in hell (10:28).

It is natural, at this point, to want to know the reason for such persecution. Why will the disciples be so hated? Why will the disciples face death? Here, we do receive an answer. Jesus constantly emphasizes that it is "because of me." Why will the disciples be dragged before councils, governors, and kings? Jesus answers, "Because of me." Why will the disciples be hated by all? Jesus answers, "Because of my name." The expected death that awaits the disciples will not be a result of their forthcoming actions, but is a result of their association with Jesus. Jesus gave the disciples authority over unclean spirits and authority to cure every disease and sickness (10:1). It is not these actions that will endanger the disciples, but rather their membership in this new group of Jesus-followers.

Jesus makes this clear. Following Jesus will tear families apart. Following Jesus will cause tension and turmoil. He explains to the disciples, "Do not think that I have come to bring peace to the earth; I have not come to bring peace, but a sword" (10:34). As if to put an exclamation point on this announcement, he outlines the brokenness that is to come to nearly every conceivable family relationship. A man will be against his own father. A daughter will be against her own mother. One's enemies will be members of one's own family (10:35–36). Jesus' words make sense in his collectivist culture, but may sound unnecessarily harsh to us, as individualists. He warns the disciples that they can only have true loyalty to one group. If they remain a member of their families, fine. But, then they are not members of his body. If they become his disciples, fine. But, then they are no longer members of their own families. He explains, "Whoever loves father or mother more than me is not worthy of me; and whoever loves son or daughter more than me is not worthy of me" (10:37). He concludes by noting, "Those who find their life will lose it, and those who lose their life for my sake will find it" (10:39). In other words, it is only when one life ends that a new life can begin.

Importantly, the message to the disciples is that this new life in Jesus does not end with persecution and death. It is true that there is a very real death to be experienced when the disciples leave their families. However, the new and unexpected life that comes by following Jesus is a life of salvation. He promises, "The one who endures to the end will be saved" (10:22). Furthermore, Jesus promises that for those that give their loyalty and devotion to him, he will give them his devotion and loyalty (10:32).

If the call of the disciples is an experience of death to life, the mission of the Twelve is also a matter of expected death and unexpected new life. Jesus warns the disciples that following him will tear families apart. Following Jesus will lead to persecution and death. However, following Jesus, with endurance and loyalty, will also mean unexpected new life and salvation.

Denial, Betrayal, and Death; Loyalty, Endurance, and Life

It is clear that throughout the gospel Jesus is accompanied by his disciples. He calls them to follow, and they follow him. He warns them of persecution, and they push onward. The disciples are a constant presence in the mission and ministry of Jesus. It is true that in many (perhaps most) of the gospel stories, the disciples seem unaware of what is *truly* happening. They do not seem to understand the meaning of Jesus' words and actions. While Jesus is teaching, the disciples are arguing over "who is the greatest in the kingdom of heaven" (18:1). But with all of their confusion and awkwardness, doubt and disbelief, the disciples are present with Jesus throughout his public ministry.

As the gospel gains momentum, building to its climactic moments, the disciples and Jesus gather together in Jerusalem for the Passover meal. While they are eating, Jesus says, "Truly I tell you, one of you will betray me" (26:21). The disciples are greatly distressed, each one saying, "Surely not I, Lord?" For us, it is not surprising to hear this from Jesus. The disciples are depicted time and time again as men "of little faith" (6:30; 8:26; 14:31; and 16:8). Furthermore, we have already been made aware of Judas' agreement to betray Jesus (26:14–16). So we are not surprised. But, we do not yet know the extent to which the disciples—all of the disciples—will betray him.

It is tempting to focus on the stories of Judas and Peter. Their stories, after all, are told in a very clear, straightforward manner. They both deny and betray Jesus. Jesus had warned his disciples earlier that they must choose their loyalties. He even said, "Everyone therefore who acknowledges me before others, I also will acknowledge before my Father in heaven; but whoever denies me before others, I also will deny before my Father in heaven" (10:32). The choice seems clear. The consequences of the choice seem clear. Perhaps this is what makes the betrayal stories, the denial stories, so engaging.

It was Judas Iscariot that went to the chief priests. It was not them that approached him. With his plan to betray Jesus in mind, he asked what they would pay him. They agreed upon the price of thirty pieces of silver (26:14–16). The amount might seem arbitrary for us. At the time, however, it was the value associated with an injured slave (Exodus 21:32; Zechariah 11:12–13). Whether we are aware of this association or not, it is clear that the price for the betrayal only hints at the offensiveness of the actual act of betrayal.

After the Passover meal, after a hymn has been sung, the disciples are with Jesus at a place called Gethsemane. Jesus, deeply anguished, deeply grieved, prays. The disciples sleep. This scene, this context, highlights the conflicted, human emotions of Jesus. The scene also highlights the growing distance between Jesus and his disciples. They are present, but they are not able to be with or support him in any meaningful way. Finally, it is Jesus himself that announces to the disciples, "Get up, let us be going. See, my betrayer is at hand" (26:46).

Judas betrays Jesus with a kiss. Artists of every age have depicted this scene. It was just days before that they were together as disciple and teacher. Just hours before that they were eating together. The kiss, a very personal expression of shared intimacy, is used to betray. The author of our gospel provides us with the end to both men's stories. For Jesus, the betrayal will lead to his crucifixion. For Judas, the betrayal will lead to his suicide (27:3–10).

Peter's denial begins with a blanket statement by Jesus: "You will all become deserters because of me" (26:31). When Peter hears these words he protests. This isn't the first time that Peter has objected to Jesus' words. Earlier, when Jesus had told his disciples that he must go to Jerusalem and undergo great suffering, it was Peter that objected. "God forbid it, Lord! This must never happen to you" (16:22). So it is again. Peter hears that all will betray Jesus, and he defends himself. "Though all become deserters because of you, I will never desert you" (26:33). With an image as memorable as Judas' kiss, Peter is told that before the cock crows he will deny Jesus three times.

There is a sense of inevitability with each story. As soon as Judas approached the chief priests with his plan, wheels were set in motion and nothing could change the course of events. With Jesus' words to Peter, the reader knows exactly what to expect in the events of that very evening. He is asked three different times by three different people if he was with Jesus of Nazareth. With each question comes the same denial of Jesus. Where Judas' betrayal led to suicide, Peter's denial sent him away weeping bitterly.

It is true that the betrayal of Judas and the denial of Peter are powerful stories. But the words of Jesus to all of the disciples cannot be lost in our reading of Matthew. Every one of the disciples would deny Jesus.

As quickly, completely, and confidently as they had followed him, they quickly, completely, and confidently deny him. The author tells us that there were many women who watched the crucifixion of Jesus from a distance. Among the women were Mary Magdalene and Mary the mother of James and Joseph. Interestingly, the gospel notes that the mother of the sons of Zebedee was also present (27:55–56). When Jesus called James and John, they left their father, Zebedee, to follow. Now, it is their mother that is present for the death of Jesus, while they have denied him.

At this point in the story, as Jesus hangs on the cross, he is alone. The disciples have abandoned Jesus. For the disciples, the death of Jesus was unexpected. With the denial and betrayal of the disciples, we witness the death of the mission and ministry of Jesus. What began with a call from Jesus has now ended with crucifixion. The group that was gathered together and given new life by Jesus is now scattered and put to death by the death of Jesus.

The burial of Jesus is not experienced by the disciples. Joseph of Arimathea, a rich man, asks for the body. He wraps it in clean linen cloth and lays it in his own new tomb. Mary Magdalene and the other Mary are there to witness the event. There is no mention of the disciples. We are not told of their location. We are not told if they are together or if they are scattered. The story is silent. With the death of Jesus, the author of Matthew also emphasizes the abandonment of the disciples.

As with the burial, the resurrection of Jesus is not experienced by the disciples. After the Sabbath, as the first day of the week was dawning, Mary Magdalene and the other Mary visit the tomb. Here, they experience a great earthquake and the appearance of an angel of the Lord. With an appearance like lightning, he announces, "Do not be afraid; I know that you are looking for Jesus who was crucified. He is not here; for he has been raised, as he said. Come, see the place where he lay. Then go quickly and tell his disciples, 'He has been raised from the dead, and indeed he is going ahead of you to Galilee; there you will see him.' This is my message to you" (28:5–7). The women leave the tomb quickly and run to tell the disciples.

The next time that we see the gathered disciples, they are on the mountain to which Jesus had directed them. They see Jesus and they worship him. We are told that they worship and doubt. Then Jesus commissions them. With words that echo their earlier commissioning in chapter 10, they are again given authority. They are given authority to make disciples of all nations. They are given authority to baptize in the name of the Father, and of the Son, and of the Holy Spirit. Finally, they are given authority to teach. With this, they again receive a promise. Jesus concludes, "Remember, I am with you always, to the end of the age" (28:16–20).

The author of Matthew ties this event together with the commissioning in chapter 10. With that commissioning, the disciples had been warned of the life that awaited the disciples. They would be persecuted and would face death. But, with loyalty and endurance, they would experience new and unexpected life and salvation. As readers, we assume that the same warning again applies to this commissioning. The road before the disciples will not be easy. The disciples will face persecution and death. But, this time, because they have experienced the risen Jesus, we have confidence that even with doubt, they will be loyal. They will have endurance. They will experience new life and salvation. And, more importantly, they will carry this message to all the nations.

Conclusion

The story of the disciples begins with call narratives that are brief. For modern readers, they seem to reveal very little about the change that is to occur in the lives of the men. It is difficult to imagine how such a simple call, "Follow me," can bring both death and new life. But the call does mean death. Family members become enemies. Leaving the family to follow Jesus will bring persecution and death. But, the call also brings unexpected new life. To follow Jesus is to belong to a new group. To follow Jesus with loyalty and endurance brings life and salvation.

The story of the disciples includes their participation in the mission and ministry of Jesus. The disciples are given authority over unclean spirits and authority to cure every disease and every sickness. However, it is not their actions that will lead to death. Rather, it is their association with Jesus that will bring hatred. It is because of his name; it is because of him that the disciples will experience death. But, it is also through their association with Jesus that they will experience new life. It is because of his name; it is because of him that that the disciples will experience salvation.

Finally, the story of the disciples includes the participation in and reactions to the death and resurrection of Jesus. The disciples, all of the disciples will deny and betray Jesus. As Jesus dies, he dies alone. The disciples abandoned him. With his death, we experience the death of his mission and ministry. The resurrection of Jesus means unexpected new life, unexpected new life not only for the risen Jesus, but also for his continuing ministry. As the disciples experience the risen Jesus, they again are commissioned. They are sent out. This time, with loyalty and endurance, they will bring the message of unexpected new life to the world.

5

Death and New Life in the Teaching of Jesus

Jesus uses both death and the cross as metaphors while teaching his disciples about the nature of faithful living. During one discussion, Jesus explains, "If any want to become my followers, let them deny themselves and take up their cross and follow me. For those who want to save their life will lose it, and those who lose their life for my sake will find it" (16:24–25). Are the words of Jesus to be understood literally? Must his followers also experience crucifixion? To be sure, Jesus has warned his disciples that they will experience suffering and even death because of him. So, it is possible that they will be forced to take up their own crosses and march to their death. However, in this case, Jesus is using both death and the cross to teach the disciples about the nature of self-denial and faithfulness.

Jesus warns his disciples that they must put to death the concerns and desires of their previous lives and live in the hope and promise that comes with their new lives in Jesus Christ. Those who cling to old ways and vain attempts at self-preservation will lose their lives. But, those who loosen their grip on previous ways and grab tightly to the call of Jesus will find new lives. In other words, those who seek to maintain their lives will find that they will actually experience loss and death. Conversely, those who give their lives up, and place their lives into the care of Jesus, will experience the promise of new life. The life of a Christ-follower, then, is a resurrected life, a new life that comes only after the death of one's previous manner of living.

Jesus is not unique in his use of death and the cross as teaching tools. The Jewish philosopher, Philo, also used the image of crucifixion when describing proper living. In a discussion of the unfortunate situation where the soul is yoked to the needs and desires of the body, he notes that "souls in this condition depend on and hang from lifeless things, for, like men crucified and nailed to a tree, they are affixed to perishable materials till they die" (*De Posteritate Caini* 61). He contrasts this situation to the soul that is wedded not to the body, but to virtue. For Philo, crucifixion is a powerful image called upon to describe a most repulsive state. Being attached to the needs of the body is like being affixed to a cross; both are shameful, both are deadly.

There are similarities in the way that both Philo and Jesus use the metaphors of death and the cross. For Philo, a soul tied to the desires of the body (a possibly tempting and temporarily appealing prospect) leads to death. Jesus explains that attempts to be in control of one's own life will actually lead to the loss of life. For both, a new and better life is only possible when one experiences the loss and death of what might seem desirable. To experience true life, unexpected new life, one must experience the death of old ways. Whether using the metaphors of death and the cross or employing other images, the theme that from death comes unexpected new life, is evident in Jesus' teaching throughout the Gospel of Matthew.

Death and New Life in the Beatitudes

The first section of Jesus' Sermon on the Mount (chapters 5–7 in the Gospel of Matthew) is commonly referred to as the "Beatitudes." These well-known sayings follow a simple pattern. Jesus proclaims, "Blessed are the . . . for they will . . ." The words sound hopeful and filled with promise. For example, "Blessed are those who mourn, for they will be comforted" (5:4). Surely, we reason, God does bless those who are experiencing loss. For modern readers, these words, taken at face value, provide comfort. But, is this all that is being emphasized? Is this all that is being taught? The Beatitudes, in their original cultural context, were a challenge to the common understanding of what was seen as honorable, to what was valued. In other words, Jesus uses as his examples people who would be understood to be dishonorable, even shameful. For example, Jesus says, "Blessed are the peacemakers, for they will be called children of God" (5:9). To *us*, this sounds fine. How could anyone challenge the honorable status of a peacemaker? However, in a world defined by honor, being a peacemaker meant something very different than what it does today. When one's honor, and the honor of the family, was being challenged, a response was deemed as more than appropriate; it was necessary. As with the honor challenge of pre-marriage pregnancy addressed earlier, a response was necessary. Such a threat to family honor often meant that an honor killing was the most "appropriate" action. In the case of a "peacemaker," this is one that would turn away from defending the family and its threatened honor. Rather than to let the situation escalate, the peacemaker steps down, or backs away from the challenge. In other words, by "keeping the peace" an individual was actually admitting defeat in this honor challenge. The peacemaker was willing to accept public shame. This was not seen as acceptable. But, in the Beatitudes, Jesus is relabeling what is honorable (or "blessed") by God.

Similarly, Jesus says that those who are "persecuted for righteousness sake" are blessed (5:10). And, "Blessed are you when people revile you and persecute you and utter all kinds of evil against you falsely on my account" (5:11). Again, Jesus is asking us to rethink what is honorable. Jesus is making a bold claim. When people view you as being shamed, God sees in you a radical version of honor. The world does not get to label you; God does. In this case, Jesus is saying that when you experience public humiliation, you are given new life in God. To show mercy to someone might not be publicly acceptable, society may turn its back on you and treat you as dead (5:7). But, you will indeed receive mercy, new life, in God. These words might sound simple, but they are not. This is a radical re-envisioning of the world. When Jesus witnesses people experiencing death, he promises new life.

Plucking Grain on the Sabbath (or, Death and New Life in God's Law)

On one particular Sabbath, Jesus was walking with his disciples through a grain field. His disciples were hungry and began to pluck heads of grain to eat. When the Pharisees saw it, they said to Jesus, "Look, your disciples are doing what is not lawful to do on the Sabbath" (12:2). Jesus responded to the challenge of the Pharisees by saying, "Have you not read what David did when he and his companions were hungry? He entered the house of God and ate the bread of the Presence, which it was not lawful for him or his companions to eat, but only for the priests. Or have you not read in the law that on the Sabbath the priests in the temple break the Sabbath and yet are guiltless? I tell you, something greater than the temple is here. But if you had known what this means, 'I desire mercy and not sacrifice,' you would not have condemned the guiltless. For the Son of Man is lord of the Sabbath" (12:3–8).

One of the great questions of the New Testament concerns the role of the laws. Did Jesus throw out the need for laws? Jesus himself said, "Do not think that I have come to abolish the law or the prophets; I have come not to abolish but to fulfill" (5:17). But what does this mean? Throughout the Gospel of Matthew, Jesus emphasizes the need for laws. In fact, in some cases Jesus seems to make the laws more difficult. When he discusses adultery, he notes, "You have heard that it was said, 'You shall not commit adultery.' But I say to you that everyone who looks at a woman with lust has already committed adultery with her in his heart" (5:27–28). In this case, the definition of adultery is broadened to incorporate not only deeds but also a wide range of thoughts and words.

According to Jesus, laws are not simply rules to be obeyed. They must be reinterpreted in the context of our many relationships. In the case of adultery, lust (taken to an extreme) can destroy a marriage commitment as surely as a physical affair. If we are called to place great respect on marriage, the broadening of the definition of adultery does not make the law more difficult. Rather, it emphasizes the importance of fidelity. In other words, if we understand laws as simply rules to follow in order to be in good standing with God and with each other, they are dead. But, if we understand laws as tools used to strengthen our relationship with God and with each other, they are alive. We control lust not because we are ordered to do so, but because we desire healthy relationships.

The case of plucking grain on the Sabbath is a great example of this transformation of death to life in the interpretation of laws. It is as if Jesus is asking the Pharisees, "Do we adhere to, follow, and respect laws, only because they have been commanded? Or, do we inquire how they impact our lives, our desire to live in community with God and with one another?" For Jesus, plucking grain on the Sabbath does not destroy our relationship with God, but it may help (in this case, in a very practical way) to strengthen our relationships with one another. In the Gospel of Matthew, to follow God's laws without attention to their implications for community is an act of death. However, to follow God's laws, paying special attention to their impact on our relationships, is an act of new life. Jesus did not come to abolish the law. In fact, we need it. Jesus did come to fulfill the law, to breathe new life into our understanding of how the law can strengthen our relationships with God and one another.

True Greatness

Jesus' disciples were concerned with greatness. On one occasion, the mother of the sons of Zebedee came to Jesus with her sons and kneeled before him. She asked Jesus to "declare that these two sons of mine will sit, one at your right hand and one at your left, in your kingdom" (20:20–22). Earlier, the disciples had asked Jesus, "Who is the greatest in the kingdom of heaven?" (18:1). The request of the mother and the question of the disciples might surprise us, but they must have seemed reasonable at the time. Jesus was concerned with status and honor and discussed repeatedly the topic of what the world honors and what God honors. In the Beatitudes, Jesus had declared that God honors and blesses those whom the world rejects. So, who is greatest in the kingdom of heaven?

When he was asked this question by his disciples, Jesus called a child before him and said, "Truly I tell you, unless you change and become like children, you will never enter the kingdom of heaven. Whoever becomes humble like this child is the greatest in the kingdom of heaven. Whoever welcomes one such child in my name welcomes me" (18:2–5). For us, as modern readers, this is a moving image. We place a tremendous value on our children. Children can be innocent and humble. They can be trusting and have simple, but powerful, expressions of faith. We reason that Jesus is asking his disciples to put away the complex issues that come with adult life and adhere to a simple and profound trust in God. Our children sing, "Jesus loves me." As adults we question, "What does it all mean?" Is Jesus asking his disciples to be more like children in our modern understanding of the term?

It is hard for us to imagine, but in the time of Jesus, children were not given the value or honor that they are today. Infant mortality was high. Children were often seen as a burden. In fact, they were typically thought of as very lowly members of the house and of society. There is evidence of this in the gospel itself. At one point, a group of little children were being brought to Jesus in order that he might lay his hands on them and pray (19:13–15). When we hear this, we imagine a loving scene. We imagine our children and grandchildren, our nieces and nephews gathered at the feet of Jesus. This is certainly how modern artists depict the event. But the response of the disciples is telling. We are told that the disciples spoke sternly to those who brought them. Jesus, however, says, "Let the little children come to me, and do not stop them; for it is to such as these that the kingdom of heaven belongs."

If children were viewed in Jesus' day as they are today, the response of the disciples would seem troubling. However, in a first-century context, their words and actions were understandable. They reasoned that Jesus does not have time for the lowest of people. But, Jesus uses this opportunity to express his understanding of true greatness. True greatness is the label given to those who have little to no social value. Where the world sees death, Jesus sees life. As the mother of the sons of Zebedee wonders who will be at Jesus' right and left hand, as the disciples wonder who will be greatest in the kingdom of heaven, Jesus provides an answer. The greatest value is given to those that we, like the disciples, often send away.

The Parable of the Lost Sheep

Jesus often teaches using parables. Through the use of short stories that employ common, everyday images, he is able to describe both the nature of God and the life of faithfulness. On one occasion, he asks his disciples, "What do you think? If a shepherd has a hundred sheep, and one of them has gone astray, does he not leave the ninety-nine on the mountains and go in search of the one that went astray?" (18:12). With this seemingly simple story, Jesus challenges his listeners to reimagine God and reimagine discipleship. This is all done within the context of expected death and unexpected new life.

In Jesus' time and place, shepherds were not respected. This was a lowest-level task that drew suspicion. Surely the sheep were eating off of other peoples' land. To ask an audience to put themselves into the place of a shepherd is already a bit of a scandal. Beyond that, this scenario has deep social implications. It is clear that Jesus is not speaking of actual shepherds and sheep. Jesus is asking a larger, more important question. How does God treat the lost? How are we to treat the lost? In this case, the description of "lost" might mean many things. Jesus describes those that society looks down upon, those without social value, as the lost. Jesus describes those that have been cast out, rejected, as the lost. Jesus describes those that have wandered, strayed, as the lost. Regardless of the specific scenario, the lost sheep represents one who is alone and is understood to have no use, no worth, no value.

Jesus continues by explaining that the shepherd goes in search of the lost sheep, and if he finds it he "rejoices over it more than over the ninety-nine that never went astray" (18:13). For some, this story seems ridiculous. Surely a shepherd does not leave ninety-nine sheep to go in search of one that is lost. What will happen to the ninety-nine? The shepherd is opening up the group to greater risk. What if they scatter? What if a wolf should come? Sometimes we must cut our losses and move on. In this case, the action of the shepherd is not to be celebrated, but is to be questioned. This is not an act of grace or mercy, but an act of foolishness. For others, this story is a story of hope and promise. It is up to the shepherd to determine the worth of the sheep. In this case, the shepherd understands the lost sheep to be of great importance, of great value. The sheep is worthy of being pursued and, when found, worthy of celebration. The perspective taken quite likely depends upon whether you understand yourself to be a member of the ninety-nine or the one that is lost.

For Jesus, this story is one of expected death and the promise of unexpected new life. By traditional standards, the lost sheep is considered dead. Whether the sheep has actually died is not the issue. The outcast, the reject, the unworthy has been lost. The ninety-nine who have followed the voice of the shepherd and who have stayed close and remained in safety are to be celebrated. But Jesus' telling of this story does not follow such traditional rules. The shepherd does pursue the lost sheep and, upon finding it, gives the sheep unexpected new life. The sheep is welcomed back and there is great rejoicing. With this telling, Jesus challenges the listeners' understanding of God; God is like a shepherd that actively pursues, finds, and celebrates the lost. Furthermore, listeners are challenged to consider what it means to be faithful. It is not only God, but all of the faithful, who are to be like this shepherd. Every Christ-follower is to seek out those who are lost, those facing death, and to bring the promise of new life that comes with being welcomed back, reunited with the others.

Dead in Sin, Alive in Forgiveness

Peter asks Jesus a question regarding forgiveness. "Lord, if another member of the church sins against me, how often should I forgive? As many as seven times?" (18:21). This question is a natural extension of the previous parable. It is one thing to welcome back one who was lost, but how many times should this occur? Is there a limit to such grace? Using a modern expression; is there a point where we conclude that "enough is enough?" To understand Peter's question, we must consider both the meaning of sin and the answer given by Jesus.

As modern readers, we might define sin as a word or a deed that breaks a rule, a law, a commandment. For Jesus, sin is necessarily interpersonal, social. Sin is that which drives a wedge between the offender and others. If we are talking about sin between individuals, sin is an action or a word that destroys a relationship. Likewise, sin is that which separates us from God. Forgiveness, then, is also a social act. To forgive someone means to repair the damage to the relationship, to bridge the gap that has been created by the destructive word or deed. If we believe (as in a modern sense), that sin is strictly defined by laws and rules and commandments, we might miss this interpersonal dynamic. We confess, "I did what I shouldn't have done, I am sorry." In contrast, when we emphasize the social reality of sin, we proclaim, "My actions have damaged our relationship. With your forgiveness, we can begin to live together, again, in community."

In this case, sin is a form of death. Where there was once a living and dynamic relationship, there is now a void. The distance between two people caused by sin is a reality that impacts every interaction. Forgiveness, then, is an act of resurrection. It is a promise of new life. Where a gulf previously existed, there is now a renewed commitment to community. So, how often should we forgive? How often should we promise to rebuild a broken relationship? Jesus says to Peter, "Not seven times, but I tell you, seventy-seven times" (18:22). In this answer, "seventy-seven" is symbolic of perfection or completeness. In other words, Jesus is saying, "Not seven times, but I tell you, *always.*"

If forgiveness is a social act, the process of repairing a broken relationship, Jesus is emphasizing that there is no limit to his promise of new life. Worded differently, we will continue to sin. In so doing, we will continue to experience death. We will continue to experience brokenness in our relationships with others and with God. But, the promise that from this death comes new life is not limited to seven times or to any other number. Rather, it is limitless and eternal. Peter (and by extension, all others who hear these words) is instructed to approach his relationships with others with a similar commitment to limitless grace, to limitless new life.

The Unforgiving Servant

In one parable, Jesus compares the kingdom of heaven to a king who wishes to settle accounts with his slaves (18:23–35). He explains that when the king began the reckoning, one slave who owed a very large sum was brought to him. However, the slave could not pay. The king ordered him to be sold, together with his wife and children and all his possessions, and for payment to be made. So the slave fell on his knees before the king, saying, "Have patience with me, and I will pay you everything." Out of pity, the king released the slave and forgave him the debt. But that same slave, as he went out, came upon one of his fellow slaves who owed him a much smaller amount. The slave seized him by the throat and said, "Pay what you owe." Then his fellow slave fell down and pleaded with him, "Have patience with me, and I will pay you." But he refused. He threw him into prison until he could pay the debt. When his fellow slaves saw what had happened, they were greatly distressed. They reported to their king all that had taken place. The king summoned the first slave and said to him, "You wicked slave! I forgave you all that debt because you pleaded with me. Should you not have had mercy on your fellow slave, as I had mercy on you?" And in anger the king handed him over to be tortured until he should pay his entire debt. Jesus concludes by explaining that "my heavenly Father will also do the same to every one of you, if you do not forgive your brother or sister from your heart."

This parable tells a double story of the transformation of death to life. To begin, the king offers a new life to the slave, who should, by all accounts, be sold or sentenced to death. The amount owed to the king was great and the king had every right to punish the slave. But the king did not do so. Rather, the king showed compassion, mercy, and grace. The king might have at least asked the slave to work off the debt. But, the king required nothing. The debt was forgiven. The second story is quite different. When the slave that had experienced the transformation of death to life encountered a fellow slave that owed him money, no grace was given.

The action of the slave is deeply troubling. It is troubling to the king, who in the parable tortures the slave. It is also troubling to Jesus, who in telling the parable emphasizes the slave's terrible lack of grace. The meaning of the story extends to every listener. Just as our debts have been forgiven, we must forgive. God expects everyone who has experienced the gracious transformation of death to life to be agents of new life.

The Disciples Have Lost Everything, but Are Promised New Life

Our last example of the transformation of death to new life in the teaching of Jesus brings our attention back to the call of his disciples. The actual calling seemed simple. Jesus said, "Follow me." And, the disciples followed Jesus. We know, however, that the call of Jesus was anything but simple. The disciples left all that they had to follow Jesus. Near the end of Jesus' ministry, Peter declared, "Look, we have left everything and followed you. What then will we have?" (19:27). Jesus replied, "Truly I tell you, at the renewal of all things, when the Son of Man is seated on the thrown of his glory, you who have followed me will also sit on twelve thrones, judging the twelve tribes of Israel. And everyone who has left houses or brothers or sisters or father or mother or children or fields, for my name's sake, will receive a hundredfold, and will inherit eternal life. But many who are first will be last, and the last will be first" (19:28–30).

The twelve had been warned by Jesus that the life of discipleship is not easy. They will suffer. They will experience death. Peter's frustrated declaration seems justified. "Look, we have left everything and followed you. What then will we have?" These words come from one who is experiencing the death that comes with discipleship. But, his situation will only grow more difficult. He will deny and abandon Jesus. But, as surely as Jesus will experience new life in the resurrection, Jesus promises new life to Peter, to all the disciples, and to all who follow him. Discipleship may mean death, but it also means the transformative power of new life.

Conclusion

In his teaching, Jesus uses images of death and new life throughout the Gospel of Matthew. At the beginning of the Sermon on the Mount, in the Beatitudes, Jesus declares that God views the world very differently than we do. Where we see shame, humiliation, and death, Jesus sees honor, blessing, and new life. Through the simple act of plucking grain on the Sabbath, Jesus asks everyone to consider again the role of the law. We are asked to see the law as life giving, breathing new life into our relationships with God and with one another. The disciples asked the same question that we often ask: "What is true greatness?" In our own pursuits of wealth and prestige, we are reminded that Jesus finds the greatest worth in the lowest members of society. Where we see death, Jesus sees life. And then there is the matter of forgiveness. How often should we forgive? Do we reflect the grace that we have received from God in our relationships with others? We have been gifted with limitless mercy. We too must strive to be agents of new life. But still we ask, "What then will we have?" Jesus promises to Peter, to his disciples, and to us, new life.

6

Physical Death and Unexpected New Life

Both the threat of death and the actual experience of death loom large throughout the Gospel of Matthew. When Jesus is still in the womb, there is a very real possibility that Mary will be killed, and Jesus with her. Making the connection between the womb and the tomb is more than an exercise in rhyming; it is a statement of just how close the two came to being one in the same. The disciples are told to expect persecution and death. Here, too, the very real possibility of death is present. In truth, death is a constant reality facing Jesus, his disciples, and all those that populate our gospel. We cannot overlook this fact, nor should we. The Gospel of Matthew addresses the reality of death head-on with words of hope. In cases where death is expected, new life may be found. In cases where death is experienced, new life is promised.

The Experience of Death in the Gospel of Matthew

The story of the birth of Jesus is followed by an account of visitors, magi from the East. The story focuses upon two themes: the praise of the magi and the jealousy of Herod. We are told that, upon entering the house, the visitors see the child with Mary, and they kneel down and pay him homage. They open treasure chests and offer him gifts of gold, frankincense, and myrrh (2:11). In sharp contrast, Herod has his own plans for the child. An angel of the Lord visits Joseph in a dream and instructs him to take the child and his mother and flee to Egypt (2:13). This is the second time in Jesus' short life that an angel intervenes as an agent of life. While Mary was pregnant with Jesus, an angel made the promise of new life known to Joseph. Here, again, an angel promises new life to Jesus.

When Herod realizes that the visitors have returned to their own country by another road and have not returned to him to report on the birth and location of the child, he is infuriated. He has been tricked. In response to this deception, Herod kills all the children in and around Bethlehem who are two years old or under. He believes that by doing so his rival will be destroyed. Here, Matthew uses words from the prophet Jeremiah to provide a very intimate description of the pain and grief. There is wailing and loud lamentation. Parents refuse to be consoled, because their children are no more (Matthew 2:18; Jeremiah 31:15).

The Gospel of Matthew invites us into the experience of Joseph and Mary. But, the gospel also invites us into the deep pain of the other parents in Bethlehem. We feel the relief of Joseph and Mary as they escape to Egypt, just as we experience the others' anguish. In this story, the theme that from expected death comes unexpected new life is emphasized. Herod indiscriminately kills all the youngest children. Jesus faces expected death. As a child in the village, he too would be killed. But from the grasp of expected death, Jesus experiences new life.

The Gospel of Matthew does not relate a single story of Jesus as a child. Rather, we move from his return from Egypt to Nazareth, when he is still very young, to his baptism by John, when he is an adult. The gospel moves quickly after the baptism of Jesus, too. He recruits disciples. He teaches. He heals the sick. And, Jesus experiences expected death. On one occasion, he gets into a boat and his disciples follow him. A windstorm arises and is so great that the boat is swamped by waves. During this, Jesus sleeps (8:23–24). This element of the story has surely captured the imagination of every reader of Matthew. It is hard (and more than a bit comical) to imagine a boat being tossed around at sea while one of its passengers sleeps through it all. The disciples are decidedly less peaceful. They wake him up, saying, "Lord, save us! We are perishing" (8:25).

This story is a helpful example of conclusion awareness. As readers of Matthew, we are aware of the death and resurrection that is to come. Therefore, we do not allow ourselves to feel the depth, the extent, of the disciples' fear. We reason, "If Jesus will conquer death and the grave, surely calming this storm is within reason." And this turns out to be the case. Jesus replies to the disciples, "Why are you afraid, you of little faith?"

Then he gets up and rebukes the winds and the sea, and there is a dead calm (8:26). We are told that the disciples are amazed. They even question, "What sort of man is this, that even the winds and sea obey him?" (8:27). The disciples may be amazed, but we as readers are not. Or, at least, we are less so. In the telling of this story, the disciples truly face expected death. They are terrified. But, more powerful than the storm is the rebuke of Jesus. The winds and waves listen to his command. And, in the midst of this expected death, the disciples experience the unexpected. They are granted new life.

In the first chapter of this book, in the introduction to the concept of conclusion awareness, we were introduced to the story of Jesus restoring the life of a girl. This may seem like a simple observation, but it is an important one: there is a difference between *resuscitation* and *resurrection*. In that story a girl who has died is brought back to life. She is resuscitated. For her, there is the very real experience of new life. However, her life has only been restored to its previous state. She will die again. At the end of the gospel, after the crucifixion of Jesus, readers are introduced to the promise of resurrection, a promise that death does not have the final word. This promise, the promise of a new resurrected life, is surely greater than that of the new life of resuscitation.

Resuscitation stories, however, are powerful. Many people, upon experiencing the death of a loved one, desire "just a little more time." We are not told the emotions of the leader of the synagogue; only that upon the death of his daughter he kneels before Jesus and says, "My daughter has just died; but come and lay your hand on her, and she will live" (9:18). This story moves us beyond *expected* death into the *experience* of death. It is one thing for Jesus to calm a storm and to offer new life in the face of expected death. It is another thing for Jesus to give new life to this girl, a girl who has experienced death.

We are told that mourners have gathered and that the crowd is making a commotion. Into this scene enters Jesus. He goes into the house and takes the girl by the hand. It is a personal, intimate description. If Jesus can calm a storm by rebuking the waves, surely he could raise this girl with words alone. But Jesus touches the girl. He takes her hand and she gets up. Just as we are not told the emotions of the father earlier in the story, we are not told of his reaction to his daughter's new life. All that we are told is that the report of this spread throughout that district (9:25–26).

Surely the report sounded something like this: "The girl was dead and is now alive. Jesus gives life to those who have died."

From the very beginning of his life, Jesus is confronted with the reality of death. Twice in his first years, an angel of the Lord appears to Joseph with words of great promise, words of new life. During their time together, Jesus and his disciples are confronted with death. Their time together will be dangerous. It will include persecution, suffering, and death. Even their daily activities can be dangerous. As the sea rages, death comes calling. In his ministry, it is not only the sick that are brought to Jesus, but Jesus is brought to those who have died. Mourners gathered around the daughter of the leader of the synagogue. When Jesus makes an announcement of new life, they laugh. But, this promise becomes a reality. Throughout Matthew, Jesus, his disciples, and those who have died receive the gift of unexpected new life.

God, Death, and Suffering

It would have been easy for our gospel writer to relate only stories of unexpected new life. After all, these are stories of power and promise. We like to watch as Jesus takes the hand of a girl who has recently died and witness her first new breath of air. We like to watch as Jesus calms a storm. We like these stories because they are immediately applicable to our lives. We have experienced the death of loved ones. We have felt lost and scared as storms rage around us. We long for the endings that these stories provide. However, these stories can also be troubling and difficult. From our experience, the dead stay dead and storms destroy homes and lives. So, what are we to make of this?

While it would have been easy for the author of our gospel to share only stories that end well, this is not what we are offered. In the Gospel of Matthew, people experience death. People grieve and feel pain and loss. At the beginning of this chapter, I outlined the unexpected new life experienced by Jesus while Herod killed all of the children in Bethlehem age two and under. We cannot help but to focus on these children. We are only told of the great grief of the parents. No explanation is given to help us understand the greater meaning or purpose for their untimely deaths. We are left to question the reason for and meaning behind this great suffering, these tragic deaths. Another such story is that of the death of John the Baptist.

The story begins with Herod's arrest of John. Herod wants to put him to death, but he fears John, for the crowds regard him as a prophet. On the event of his birthday, the daughter of his wife dances before Herod and all of his guests. Herod is so pleased that he promises to grant her whatever she might ask. Prompted by her mother, she says, "Give me the head of John the Baptist here on a platter" (14:8). The king is grieved, yet out of regard for his oath, John is beheaded in prison. The head of John is brought on a platter and given to the girl. After the death, the disciples take the body and bury it, and Jesus is told all what has happened (14:1–12).

When Jesus hears of the death of John, he withdraws to a deserted place by himself (14:13). We are not told what Jesus is thinking or feeling. We are not told anything about Jesus' grief or pain or loss. We are only told that he withdraws to be alone. And, worded crassly, John stays dead. In this case, there is no experience of resuscitation. Sure the two deaths differ. John has been, after all, beheaded. But, couldn't Jesus also make John live again? So, why doesn't he do it? The stories of death in the Gospel of Matthew sit uncomfortably close to the stories of new life. We can't help but ask, "Why do some people experience new life while others do not?"

For this chapter, and for our reading of the Gospel of Matthew, we must acknowledge that the gospel does not provide a systematic explanation for suffering and death. In other words, our author does not provide that which many of us so desperately want. We are not given an answer to the question, "Why?" "Why do we experience suffering?" However, what the author of the gospel does provide is important. The Gospel of Matthew does not shy away from the reality of suffering and death. The author acknowledges that this is a very real part of our life and faith experience. Furthermore, the gospel proclaims, in no uncertain terms, that God has power over death; that in the face of death, God promises unexpected new life.

The Crucifixion and Death of Jesus

The crucifixion of Jesus is the most powerful, vivid story of physical death in the Gospel of Matthew. Jesus hangs from a cross stained with his own blood. Even from a government known for its displays of brutality, this form of capital punishment is extreme. The death of Jesus is so real, so powerful, that it is described with cataclysmic details. The sky turns dark and the earth shakes (27:45, 51). There is no question that Jesus is dead. To understand this story of grotesque death, we must examine the practice of crucifixion itself. It can be said with certainty that Jesus was crucified. However, the details of his crucifixion (and crucifixion in general) remain a bit of a mystery. What do we know about the physical death of Jesus?

It may surprise modern readers, but very little was written by ancient authors regarding crucifixion. While we know that this practice occurred throughout the Roman Empire, sometimes with great frequency, it was a topic that writers seemed to avoid. We could speculate on why this might be. But our guesses would be just that—guesses. In the end, what we must acknowledge is that we have relatively little literary evidence concerning this method of murder. In fact, the gospel accounts of the crucifixion of Jesus are the most detailed, thorough descriptions available today. So, it is there that we begin.

In the Gospel of Matthew, the crucifixion of Jesus begins with him being flogged, or whipped (27:26). Next, Jesus is mocked. He is dressed like a king, complete with a crown of thorns, and spat upon and beaten with a stick (27:29–30). Finally, Roman soldiers lead Jesus away to be crucified. Here, we are told that a man from Cyrene named Simon is forced to carry the cross of Jesus. When they reach the place called Golgotha (or "Place of the Skull"), Jesus is crucified. He is not, however, crucified alone. Two bandits flank him. To be sure, his crucifixion is not private. People pass by Jesus (27:39–40). Chief priests, scribes, and elders mock, "He saved others. He cannot save himself" (27:42). Even the bandits taunt him in the same way (27:44). While his disciples have fled, others are there to witness his death. He breathes his last around three o'clock. Since we do not know when he was crucified, we do not know how long he endured this terrific agony. That is all that we are told in our gospel regarding the crucifixion of Jesus.

Is Matthew's description of the crucifixion of Jesus consistent with what we know from other sources? What is known from ancient literature and archaeology? To begin, it does seem that torture and flogging was common before crucifixion. While this act of torture was common, there was not a uniform practice. For example, the instruments used in whipping varied, as did the extent of the abuse. In fact, it is reported that many people died during the torture and were never crucified. Matthew's description of the flogging of Jesus, then, is consistent with known Roman practices during the first century.

To imagine this element of our story, we must be aware that crucifixion was always a public form of execution and occurred outside of the city gates. Because it was not a rare occurrence, the uprights of the crosses were likely permanent fixtures. Those to be crucified would be made to carry a crossbeam along with a notice of the crime that was committed. When the condemned man, bloodied from being flogged, arrived at the site of execution, he was tied or nailed to the crossbeam and with it was lifted into place upon the permanent post. It is not hard to imagine, therefore, that Jesus, so badly injured from flogging, needed assistance carrying his crossbeam.

While the entire gospel builds to the crucifixion of Jesus, the actual event receives no description. The lack of information reminds us, again, of the birth of Jesus. There is no description of his birth. We are not told the time or the location. We are not told whether or not there were witnesses. Were women gathered to assist with the delivery? In the first chapter of Matthew, we are simply told that he was born and that Joseph named him Jesus (1:25). The crucifixion of Jesus receives a similar treatment. In English, the actual event does not even constitute a full sentence (27:35). What did this scene look like? Artists through the centuries have attempted to fill in the missing details. How tall was the cross? What was its shape? It is important to note that while the act of crucifixion was common, the manner in which it was carried out varied greatly. Just as there was no uniformity in torture, there was no consistency in crucifixion. Rather, the manner of death was at the whim of the executioner. We know that many crosses were relatively short, so that the one being crucified was very near to the ground. This made it easier for dogs to rip the body from the cross when the execution was finished. We know that the shape of crosses varied. In the end, we simply do not know what the cross or the scene looked like.

Finally, we are told that there were many witnesses to Jesus' crucifixion. Matthew's gospel says that people passed by and mocked Jesus as he hung on the cross. The Jewish philosopher Philo describes the crucifixion of Jews in Alexandria as a form of popular entertainment. There a person was crucified only after being flogged in the middle of the theater and being tortured with fire and sword (*In Flaccum* 84). Elsewhere, crucifixion is compared to the public nature, and even public entertainment, of other forms of capital punishment, such as victims being fed to wild animals. The very location of the act meant that it was intended for public viewing. Crosses were positioned just outside of the busy city gate. We can only imagine (and, perhaps we cannot imagine) the type of ridicule that a criminal would receive from hardened onlookers.

A bit more is known about the practice of crucifixion. For example, Roman citizens could be crucified, but this was rare. In very special cases of serious crime or treason, citizens could be sentenced to this form of death. Crucifixion was typically reserved for non-citizens. Furthermore, this was a death that often signaled a crime or threat against the state. Finally, crucifixion was a typical punishment for slaves. In other words, the crucifixion of a non-Roman citizen from Nazareth who was understood to be a threat to the state is consistent with known Roman practices.

Since little was written about crucifixion in the ancient world, it should come as no surprise that little was written about the burial of those crucified. It has been argued by some that since Jesus died as a criminal, he would not have received a formal burial. However, we know that Jewish custom did permit those who had been condemned to death under Roman law could be buried in family tombs. In fact, the only known archaeological evidence of crucifixion, a crucified ankle bone, was found in a rock-cut family tomb in Jerusalem.

The story of the death of Jesus is told succinctly, with little detail. Jesus is flogged, mocked, killed, and buried. Every element of this story is consistent with known Roman practices. As with most stories of Jesus, we would like to know more. Yet, the singular intent of the story is clear: Jesus is truly, physically, dead.

Resurrection as a Physical Reality

Just as the crucifixion and death of Jesus is a brutal physical reality, the resurrection and new life of Jesus is a physical reality. Jesus is truly, physically alive. This is important. The author of the Gospel of Matthew does not confuse resuscitation with resurrection and, as readers, we must not either. There are two important elements, or dynamics, to the promise of resurrection. First, as surely as death is physical, resurrection is physical. Second, whereas resuscitation is a return to one's old life, the resurrected life is an altogether new experience.

Our gospel emphasizes the physical reality of the resurrection. Immediately following his death, we are told that Jesus is placed in a new tomb, hewn in rock, and that a great stone is rolled in front of the entrance (27:60). There are witnesses to the reality of this death and burial. Mary Magdalene and the other Mary sit opposite the tomb, watching the entire event unfold (27:61). The Sabbath passes and, as the first day of the week is dawning, the same witnesses return to the site. Mary Magdalene and the other Mary go to see the tomb. Suddenly, there is a great earthquake and an angel of the Lord descends from heaven. The angel rolls back the stone from the tomb and sits on it. The angel says to the women, "Do not be afraid; I know that you are looking for Jesus who was crucified. He is not here; for he has been raised" (28:5–6). The empty tomb is visible to the women. Just as surely as they witnessed Jesus' body in the tomb and the stone rolled in place, they now witness the stone rolled away and the tomb empty. The gospel emphasizes that just as surely as the burial was physical, the resurrection is physical. "He is not here."

The resurrected body, the resurrection life, is physical. However, this experience is not described as a simple return to a previous state, the old life. The resurrected body, the resurrection life, is one that has been transformed. Jesus appears suddenly to the women and later to his disciples. Announcing himself, using the same words as the angels, Jesus declares, "Do not be afraid." They are not witnessing a body that has been brought back to life, as Jesus had done to the daughter of the leader of the synagogue. They are witnessing the resurrected Jesus. And what do they do when they see him? They worship him; but some doubt (28:17).

Conclusion

Death is a physical reality. And, the Gospel of Matthew takes seriously this reality. In some cases, unexpected new life is experienced by those facing death. As Jesus and his disciples are tossed about by the sea, and death is expected, Jesus acts as the agent of new life. Jesus calms the storm and unexpected new life is granted. In some cases, unexpected new life is experience by those who have died. We watch as mourners surround the daughter of the leader of the synagogue who has died. Her death is not expected, not forthcoming; it has already happened. But, just as real as the death itself is the reality of new life granted to her by the touch of Jesus. She is resuscitated. In the midst of her death comes unexpected new life.

The experience of death, however, does not always end in this way. In our gospel (and in our own lives) physical death is a reality. The parents in Bethlehem grieve, with great cries, after the slaughter of their children. Jesus goes off alone to grieve after the death of John the Baptist. But even here, even when death seems to have had the final word, the story is not over. In the death and resurrection of Jesus, a new reality is declared, a new promise is given: *from expected death comes unexpected new life.*

7

Social Death and Unexpected New Life

mmediately following the Sermon on the Mount, a great crowd follows Jesus. A leper comes before him, kneels down and says, "Lord, if you choose, you can make me clean." Jesus stretched out his hand and touched him, saying, "I do choose. Be made clean" (8:1–4). This story is short, simple, and few details are provided. There is a crowd, a leper, and Jesus. But it is the economy of language that drives home the central image and intended meaning. The leper is not part of the crowd. The crowd is not described. But, we may assume that they are travelling together, huddled close, touching. The crowd is great. They are talking, perhaps laughing. By telling us nothing about the crowd, the author tells us everything that we need to know: they are acting as one. In this story they are, together, one character. The leper, on the other hand, is not a part of the crowd. The leper is unclean. The leper is alienated and alone. Where the crowd accepts one another, they reject the leper. This story describes a kind of death: social death. This story also describes a kind of resurrection, reminding us that from social death comes unexpected new life.

What Is Social Death?

Social death refers to the experience of an individual that has been rejected by his or her social group; the experience that accompanies being defined as deviant, impure, and cast out. Such rejection can, but does not always, result in physical death. In the deeply group-oriented culture of the first century, to be removed from one's group, one's family, meant that there was no social support. When home, work, relationships, and protection are taken away, death was often the result. However, social death ought not to be understood as a step toward the worse event of physical death. In fact, physical death could be understood as relief from the agony of social death. To be deemed unworthy, unacceptable, permanently flawed and to be treated with contempt is a form of death known by some in the Gospel of Matthew.

It may be helpful at this point to note that there is both a *physical* element and a *social* element to every discussion of disease. The *physical* element refers to the pathological condition of an organ or system resulting from various causes, such as infection or genetic defect, and is identified by a group of signs or symptoms. In the example above, the "leper" surely had some type of skin condition. We could discuss the pathological condition of the leper. We could inquire about the possible causes for skin disease in first-century Galilee. And we could speculate on the symptoms present. In contrast, the *social* element reflects the reality that disease changes the value of the individual within the social group. When an individual is labeled as diseased, the place, or role, of the individual in the social group is redefined. Referring again to the example above, the leper does have a pathological condition; a skin disease. However, he has also been labeled as impure. His condition is seen as a threat to the social group. His value has been redefined. In this case, he is rejected.

Just as any discussion of disease has both a physical and social component, the discussion of care has both a physical and social element. Regarding the physical element, a *cure* eliminates the pathological condition. With the example of leprosy, a cure would eliminate the skin disease. Regarding the social element, to *heal* is to re-evaluate, redefine, and restore the value, or worth, of individuals to their previous place in the social group. With leprosy, healing the individual is a social process; it is to reintegrate the individual into the group.

So, what does Jesus do? Is Jesus interested in the *physical* or the *social*? Does Jesus *cure* or *heal*? Our short story of Jesus, the crowd, and the leper offers an interesting perspective. We are told that after he is approached by the leper, Jesus says, "Be made clean!" Immediately the leprosy is cleansed. This is an act of curing the disease. With these words, "Be made clean," the pathological skin condition has been eliminated. But, this is not the end of the story. Jesus also says, "See that you say nothing to anyone; but go, show yourself to the priest, and offer the gift that Moses commanded, as a testimony to them" (8:1–4). Here, Jesus is engaging in the act of healing. The man, previously defined by his leprosy, still needs to be redefined, or relabeled, as "clean." The formal, or official, act of relabeling the man as clean is the job of the priest. When the man presents himself to the priest and makes the appropriate offering, he will be defined as clean and will be welcomed back into the group. In other words, Jesus takes great care to offer both a physical cure and social healing. In the case of this man, living with the reality of social death, Jesus offers unexpected new life.

Social Death in the Gospel of Matthew

A helpful place to begin our consideration of social death in Matthew's gospel is near the end of Jesus' ministry. Just before Jesus' triumphal entry into Jerusalem, he heals two blind men. We are told that just as Jesus and his disciples were leaving Jericho, a large crowd followed him. There were two blind men sitting by the roadside. The two men heard that Jesus was passing by and shouted, "Lord, have mercy on us, Son of David" (20:29–30). This story is very similar to the previous narrative with a crowd and a leper. In both, a crowd is juxtaposed with an outcast. Neither story describes the crowd, indicating that what the members of the crowd do have in common is their shared disregard for the outcast. This story, however, offers a very telling detail. When the crowd hears the men shouting to Jesus, they respond. The crowd sternly ordered them to be quiet (20:31). In other words, not only does the "disease" of blindness prevent them from seeing, it also prevents them from being included in the crowd. In addition, the crowd believes that the men's blindness should also prevent them from experiencing the healing grace of Jesus. The "disease," then, is physical. The men cannot see. But, it is much more. The "disease" is social. Their blindness means that they are have been labeled as deviants and have been cast out of the group. The crowd assumes that Jesus will also understand the men to be impure, devalued. The crowd reasons that if they have rejected the blind men, surely Jesus will do the same.

But, the blind men continue to shout even more loudly, "Have mercy on us Lord, Son of David!" (20:31). Upon hearing this, Jesus stands still. He calls to them, asking, "What do you want me to do for you?" To modern readers, this question seems quite odd. Why would Jesus ask such a question? Surely the men want Jesus to restore their sight. And, the men do reply, "Lord, let our eyes be opened" (20:33). But, this request has both physical and social consequences. Jesus, we are told, is moved with compassion and touches their eyes. Immediately they regain their sight. A physical cure is offered; the men regain their sight. But, in so doing, a social healing is also provided. With sight, that which separated the men from the crowd has been removed.

Another story begins with some people carrying a paralyzed man lying on a bed. In this case, the man is not alone, but has a small group of people interested in his well-being. When Jesus sees the faith of those carrying the man, he says to the paralytic, "Take heart, son; your sins are forgiven" (9:2). To our modern ears these words might seem troubling. Is Jesus saying that the man is paralyzed because he has sinned? If so, what does this mean for our own understanding of sin and suffering? We do not look at those who are paralyzed and ask, "What sin has caused your paralysis?" So, what are we to make of these words? In this case, Jesus is addressing the social dynamic of paralysis. Jesus is relabeling the man as one who is clean, forgiven, pure, acceptable to others. In other words, Jesus is not offering a cure. There is no mention (at this point) of the man getting up or walking. There is no mention that the paralysis has been eliminated. Rather, Jesus has made a social statement, "Your sins are forgiven."

After his declaration of forgiveness, some scribes say to themselves, "This man is blaspheming." In other words, Jesus is doing what only God can do. In this case, it is only God that can redefine, relabel, a sinner as "forgiven." Only God can invite a sinner back into the community of the righteous. But Jesus perceives the thoughts of the scribes and says, "Why do you think evil in your hearts? For which is easier, to say, 'Your sins are forgiven,' or to say, 'Stand up and walk?'" (9:5). Here, Jesus makes very clear the distinction between *healing* and *curing*, between the *social* and the *physical* dynamics of disease. Which is easier, to tear down the social barriers that separate the paralyzed man from all others, or to cure his paralysis? Like most questions asked by Jesus, there is no simple answer available to the scribes. It is, of course, easier to say that someone is forgiven. It is easier to say that there is nothing that separates the paralyzed man from the scribes and the others. But, the scribes know this is not true. No matter what one says, there are still very real social implications to being paralyzed. While the scribes consider this question, Jesus continues. "But so that you may know that the Son of Man has authority on earth to forgive sins," he then said to the paralytic, "Stand up, take your bed and go to your home" (9:6). In other words, Jesus cured the man's paralysis in order to prove that he also has the power and authority to heal. It is as if he is saying, "See, if I can cure someone, surely I can relabel, redefine, that one as worthy to be a part of the group."

The reason that this story is so interesting is that it highlights a central truth to the concept of social death. We might think that physical death is much worse than social death. Likewise, we might think that curing the physical disease is much more difficult than healing, or removing, a social barrier. But, for those who have experienced any form of social alienation, for those who have been labeled as "unworthy," the reality of this experience is not only very painful, but also is very difficult to heal. Recall Jesus' challenge: which is easier, to say, "You are one of us," or "You are physically healed?" It is easier to *say* that social barriers have been removed, but it is much more difficult to actually *live* as if this is the case, to live as if this is true. In this story, and throughout the Gospel of Matthew, Jesus addresses the reality of social death. Jesus relabels those who have been deemed impure. Jesus includes the outcast.

Our awareness of both the physical and the social components of disease necessarily changes the way we read Matthew. For example, stories that otherwise seem short and lacking in detail are now much more rich with meaning. We are told that after Jesus had fed five thousand and had crossed the Sea of Galilee, he and his disciples reached Gennesaret. The people of that place recognize him and send word throughout the region. They bring their sick to Jesus. They beg to touch even the fringe of his cloak that they may be healed (14:34–36). With just three verses and no attention given to a single individual or illness, it would be tempting to move quickly past this account. But, this is no longer an option. We can imagine the physical reality of disease. This alone may spark compassion in us as readers. But, we now can also imagine the social reality of disease. The nameless and faceless men and women are now people who are seeking *healing*. They no longer wish to be referred to as "sick." And, in their experience of social death, Jesus offers unexpected new life.

Crucifixion and Social Death

In the last chapter, I explained that the crucifixion of Jesus is the most powerful, vivid example of physical death in the Gospel of Matthew. This is most certainly true. However, the crucifixion of Jesus is also the most powerful example of social death in our gospel. Crucifixion was a most gruesome tool of physical death. There is no way to read the story without being shocked by the brutality of this means of execution. Likewise, there is no way to read the account of the death of Jesus without being offended by the statement that is being proclaimed. Jesus is being shamed and mocked. The crucifixion was not only a tool of death; it was a public statement of one's social worth (or the lack thereof). So, what do we know about the social death of Jesus?

Our discussion of the social death of Jesus begins with his trial. After his arrest, Jesus is brought before the high priest and questioned. We are told that Jesus is brought to the house of Caiaphas, where the scribes and elders are gathered. Caiaphas, the high priest, says, "I put you under oath before the living God, tell us if you are the Messiah" (26:63). Jesus answers, "You have said so. But I tell you, from now on you will see the Son of Man seated at the right hand of Power and coming on the clouds of heaven" (26:64). With these words, the high priest announces that Jesus has blasphemed. The crowd delivers their verdict: "He deserves death" (26:66). It is at this point that Jesus undergoes his first experience of degradation. The crowd spits in his face and strikes him. Some slap Jesus, saying, "Prophesy to us, you Messiah! Who is it that struck you?" (26:67).

The actions of the high priest, the scribes, and the elders are a direct challenge to the status of Jesus. They are publicly mocking him and challenging his honor. With this, the relabeling of Jesus has begun. Earlier in the gospel, we listened as Peter proclaimed, "You are the Messiah, the Son of the living God" (16:16). Now, Peter watches from the courtyard as Jesus is spat upon. Furthermore, the label "Messiah" is now used sarcastically to ridicule Jesus.

The degradation of Jesus continues with his trial before Pilate. While Pilate questions Jesus, "Do you not hear how many accusations they make against you?" Jesus remains silent. This silence amazes Pilate. Next, we are told that at the festival of the Passover the governor was accustomed to releasing a prisoner to the crowd; anyone they chose. The story emphasizes the challenge being made to the honor of Jesus. The crowd will be given the choice to emphatically declare their evaluation of the worth of Jesus. So, Pilate asks, "Whom do you want me to release for you, Jesus Barabbas or Jesus who is called the Messiah?" (27:16). With this question, Pilate is asking the crowd whether they value the life of a known criminal over the life of Jesus, who has been falsely accused. In case the social dynamic is missed by readers, the gospel itself explains that Pilate "realized that it was out of jealousy that they had handed him over" (27:18). In other words, this "trial" does not reflect the guilt or innocence of Jesus; it is a process of social labeling. The crowd will be given the opportunity to publicly humiliate Jesus.

This is precisely what occurs. The crowd says that they wish for Barabbas to be released. Subsequently, Pilate asks, "Then what should I do with Jesus who is called the Messiah?" (27:22). With this question, Pilate not only places the life of Jesus into the hands of the crowd, he also places the social worth of Jesus into their hands. With this power, they say, "Let him be crucified" (27:22). The shouts to crucify Jesus are most certainly a death sentence. These words will lead to his physical death. However, the shouts are also words of social labeling. The crowd is rejecting Jesus.

After the "trial" of Jesus (or, better worded, after this public declaration of rejection), soldiers take Jesus into Pilate's headquarters and gather a crowd around him. The soldiers strip him and put a scarlet robe on him. By placing a scarlet robe on Jesus, the soldiers are mocking his supposed royal status. Next, the soldiers twist some thorns into a crown and put it on his head. The crown of thorns is another example of how the crucifixion of Jesus is both physical and social in nature. The crown most certainly brings terrible physical pain to Jesus. This crown rips his skin. However, the crown is also a social statement. With this symbol, the crowd is proclaiming that the only crown that Jesus is worthy to wear is a crown of shame and mockery. The soldiers put a reed in the right hand of Jesus and kneel before him. Remember, Jesus has already been flogged and beaten. He is covered in blood. The physical agony is terrific. Kneeling before Jesus makes a strong statement. "You will soon be dead. You have been rejected. You cannot stop what is about to happen. You have no power, no honor. You are *not* a king."

Crucifixion itself is a social statement. Rome used quicker, less painful, less public, and less shameful methods of execution. For example, hanging was considered a lesser penalty. Of course, both methods of execution ultimately have the same result. But, hanging does not have the same physical or social implications as crucifixion. While there were a very few exceptions, crucifixion was largely reserved for slaves and non-Romans. In other words, the very act of crucifixion emphasized that the one being killed was an "outsider." Likewise, crucifixion was reserved for the lowest class. Again, the one being killed was quickly identified as lacking any of the social worth that might lead to a more dignified death. In our gospel, Jesus is crucified with two bandits, one on his right and one on his left. The inclusion of this detail makes clear that in death, Jesus is in the company of (and is the social equivalent to) criminal outcasts. Our author even tells us that these bandits taunted him. This is surely meant to serve as an exclamation point to the story. Jesus is viewed with contempt and dishonor even by those without honor.

The location of the crucifixion is also ripe with social implications. Crucifixions were held outside of the city gates. This is important for two reasons. First, being outside of the gate was a statement of rejection and abandonment. Even in death (or, especially in death) Jesus is declared unclean, impure, and unworthy of inclusion. Second, while the execution was outside of the city gates, this was a very visible location. In other words, this was a high-traffic, high-profile location. Many people could and would observe this public shame. The Gospel of Matthew emphasizes this social dynamic. Our author notes that those who passed by derided him, shaking their heads and saying, "You would destroy the temple and build it in three days, save yourself! If you are the Son of God, come down from the cross" (27:40).

Little can be said regarding the actual crucifixion itself. The shape of the crosses used varied. The height of crosses varied. There is, however, an element of the story that can be assumed: Jesus was naked. Simply stated, every element of this means of execution was meant to shame, to mock, and to ridicule. While artists commonly depict Jesus wearing some sort of clothing, this is likely not a historical reality. The cross was truly a tool of humiliation.

The crucifixion of Jesus was physical. But, our author tells us little about the physical aspect of Jesus' death. In sharp contrast, the Gospel of Matthew goes to great lengths to emphasize the social death of Jesus. Jesus has been betrayed, denied, and abandoned by every one of the twelve of his disciples. His trial is not concerned with truth, with guilt or innocence, but is an occasion for public rejection. He is spat upon, mocked, dressed like a king, and "worshipped." He is crucified with social outcasts.

Onlookers address him with scorn. He is naked. The crucifixion of Jesus is the ultimate example of social labeling. Jesus is completely rejected. As Jesus dies a physical death, he also experiences complete social alienation, social death.

Social Death, Resurrection, and Unexpected New Life

Our discussion of social death has included two unique expressions of alienation described in the Gospel of Matthew. First, we have considered the social death that may accompany physical disease. For example, we have witnessed the social death experienced by those with leprosy. Second, we have considered the social death that is experienced by Jesus in his trial and crucifixion. In both cases, our gospel writer emphasizes that from social death comes unexpected new life.

How does our gospel highlight the promise of unexpected new life for those experiencing the social death that may accompany physical disease? To begin, the gospel makes a distinction between acts of *curing* and acts of *healing*. Jesus most certainly cares for the physical well-being of those around him. Stories of curing are numerous in the Gospel of Matthew. When Jesus enters Capernaum, a Roman centurion comes to him, saying, "Lord, my servant is lying at home paralyzed, in terrible distress" (8:5–6). After talking with the centurion, Jesus is impressed with his faith. In that very hour, the servant is cured. Immediately following this event, Jesus enters Peter's house. He sees Peter's mother-in-law lying in bed with a fever. Jesus touches her hand and the fever leaves her (8:14–15). The examples of Jesus' concern for physical health are many. Jesus stops the bleeding of a woman who has been hemorrhaging for twelve years (9:20–22). Jesus enters a synagogue on a Sabbath. There is a man there with a withered hand. The people gathered ask him, "Is it lawful to cure on the Sabbath" (12:9–10)? Jesus emphasizes that it is indeed lawful to do good on the Sabbath and he cures the man. There are many such stories and each emphasizes that Jesus can and does cure physical disease. However, our gospel writer emphasizes Jesus' concern for the outcast, for those experiencing social death, for those longing to be *healed*.

In the Gospel of Matthew, Jesus is concerned with the alienation experienced by those that are rejected, labeled as impure, those who are cast out. In some cases, it is not enough to cure the physical disease. What is most needed is the invitation to rejoin the group. What is most needed

is to be relabeled, to be recategorized as clean, acceptable. This invitation
to rejoin the social group is an invitation to new life. Social death is a very
real form of death. To be stripped of social worth and viewed as a threat is
to experience social death. However, healing is the act of reassigning social worth. Healing is an act of social resurrection. Where there was once
rejection, alienation, and death, there is now acceptance, expressions of
community, and life. In other words, the Gospel of Matthew proclaims
unexpected new life to those experiencing social death.

The second example of social death in the Gospel of Matthew is
that which was experienced by Jesus in his trial and crucifixion. The trial
of Jesus was not a trial concerned with truth, with guilt or innocence.
The trial of Jesus was an opportunity to mock, shame, and reject Jesus.
Similarly, the crucifixion of Jesus was not only a means of physical execution; it was also a means of social death. As Jesus hung naked on the cross,
he was exposed to public humiliation and disgrace. Even those crucified
with him rejected him. The gospel, in turn, describes the resurrection in
terms of both its physical reality and its social implications. In short, the
resurrection of Jesus is described as a social reality, as an experience of
unexpected new life.

There are hints of social relabeling immediately following the death
of Jesus. While he has been abandoned by all of his disciples, he is not
completely alone. After Jesus has died, a rich man from Arimathea named
Joseph comes to Pilate and asks for the body. The body that only a few
hours earlier was dressed and mocked as a king, complete with crown of
thorns, is now retrieved for burial. Jesus' body is wrapped in clean linen
clothes and laid in the Joseph's own new tomb. This sign of respect, and
even reverence, stands in sharp contrast to the treatment he experienced
on the cross. In addition, this treatment begins the process of relabeling
Jesus. For Joseph of Arimathea, Jesus is worthy of this honorable burial.

While Jesus was denied and abandoned by each of his twelve disciples, he was not completely alone at the time of his death or burial.
From a distance, a group of women observed Jesus on the cross. Mary
Magdalene, Mary the mother of James and Joseph, and the mother of the
sons of Zebedee were present when he died. Likewise, Mary Magdalene
and the other Mary sat opposite the tomb when Jesus was buried. Jesus,
in other words, had not been stripped of all of his social value. There
were a small number who were present to grieve his death. After the
Sabbath, as the first day of the week was dawning, Mary Magdalene

and the other Mary went to see the tomb. Just as Joseph of Arimathea honored Jesus with a burial, the women honored Jesus with this visit to his tomb. With these events, readers are assured that Rome could not completely strip Jesus of his social worth. He is physically dead. He has experienced terrific social rejection. But, for some, even in death, Jesus is still worthy of honor.

Where the actions of Joseph of Arimathea and the women were modest, the resurrection of Jesus is told as a complete social vindication. Not only has Jesus experienced physical new life, but he must be relabeled. His social worth must be re-evaluated. The resurrection, in other words, is a rebuttal to all that was said and done by the crowd. Where they mocked him as a false king, the resurrection proves his true royal status. We are told that after witnessing the empty tomb, the women experience the risen Jesus. He says to them, "Greetings" (28:9). The women take hold of his feet and worship him. With their gesture of reverence, the false worship offered by the soldiers and the crowd is reversed, negated. Now, the true status of Jesus is revealed. He is worthy of worship. The experience of the disciples is similar to that of the women. When the eleven see Jesus they worship him. Jesus, who was rejected, is now accepted. Jesus, who was deemed unworthy of praise, is now worshipped. In the resurrection, Jesus is truly alive. In the resurrection, the true status of Jesus is revealed.

Conclusion

With a story that juxtaposes a leper with a crowd, the Gospel of Matthew addresses both the reality of physical disease and its social implications. With the story of two blind men and another crowd, the gospel addresses the reality of the rejection and alienation that is experienced by some with physical diseases. Our gospel asks whether it is easier to cure the physical disease or to heal the social death that often precedes the physical one. Jesus does cure physical illness. However, his actions of healing social wounds are equally important in our gospel. Jesus shows great concern for those who have been alienated and rejected. Furthermore, Jesus invites the outcast back into the social group. Jesus provides unexpected new life to those experiencing social death.

The resurrection of Jesus is also told as a reversal of social value. Jesus, like many before him, was rejected. Jesus was mocked and stripped of honor. In his resurrection, however, his true value is made known.

Jesus is worthy of worship. The resurrection, then, is a powerful example of relabeling and re-evaluation. When crucifixion seems to be the end of the story, the resurrection has the last word. It is with glory and honor that this story ends.

8
Great Commission

The Continuing Story of Unexpected New Life

The Gospel of Matthew ends with a call to mission. This should not surprise us. Jesus called his disciples and trained them for mission. They were given authority over unclean spirits and were given the power to cure every disease and sickness (10:1). Jesus warned the disciples that their call would not be easy; it would include great suffering and even death. What might come as a surprise is that just as quickly as the disciples abandoned him, the eleven remaining disciples (Judas hanged himself; 27:5) gathered together around the resurrected Jesus. The gospel does not tell us where the disciples were during the death and burial of Jesus. It only stresses that they were not present for his last hours. As surely as Jesus had died, the mission of the Twelve seemed over. However, the angel whom the women encountered at the empty tomb instructed the women to go to the disciples and tell them that Jesus has been raised from the dead. They quickly departed and told the disciples this good news. The end of Matthew's gospel moves straight from the good news of the resurrection to a new call, a new commission, new instructions for mission.

Gathered in Galilee on the mountain to which Jesus had directed them, the disciples encountered the risen Jesus. They saw him and they worshipped him. We are told that some doubted. Nothing more is said about this doubt; the story simply moves to Jesus' words. "All authority in heaven and on earth has been given to me. Go therefore and make disciples of all nations, baptizing them in the name of the Father and of the Son and of the Holy Spirit, and teaching them to obey everything that I have commanded you. And remember, I am with you always, to the end of the age" (28:18–20). With this bold charge, the Gospel of Matthew comes to a close.

From Genealogy to New Commission

The Gospel of Matthew begins with a genealogy, a list of names beginning with Abraham and ending with Jesus. The gospel ends with a call to mission. At first, the two may seem far removed from one another. What does the Jesus family tree have to do with these words of instruction? They are separated by time, with the life, ministry, death, and resurrection of Jesus experienced between the two. And, they are separated by literary style. A list of names and a narrative are certainly different from one another. But the two are connected in very important ways. Understanding one helps to understand the other. They serve as appropriate bookends to this powerful story.

As we previously discovered, the genealogy is much more than merely a list of names. The genealogy is an account of faithfulness stretching from Abraham to Jesus. This serves to establish that the life of Jesus is to be understood as being part of a long line of faithfulness. In other words, the story does not begin with Jesus. In fact, the gospel stretches back to the earliest stories of our Bible. Abraham was faithful to God. Isaac and Jacob were faithful to God. David was faithful to God. Even the names we might not be as familiar with are included for a reason. They tell us God was working through generations, three sets of fourteen generations. Faith was passed along in Jesus' family tree. The genealogy also tells the stories of four women. In each case, the family and its very faithfulness faced expected death. Each woman, however, breathed new life, unexpected new life, into the family and its story of faithfulness. In other words, Jesus was born into a long line of men and women who were faithful to God. Jesus was also born into a long line of men and women who had experienced the unexpected new life that comes only from God. Jesus, however, is not simply another name to be added to this genealogy. Jesus serves as the ultimate example of faithfulness. Furthermore, the life and death of Jesus serves as the ultimate proclamation that from expected death comes unexpected new life.

The commission that comes at the end of the gospel is a call to continue this "faith genealogy." Jesus commands the eleven to "make disciples of all nations." In other words, they are to take the faith that began with Abraham, and has now been forever redefined by Jesus, and pass it along to all the world. The end of Matthew's gospel is a proclamation to make new faith genealogies, genealogies that proclaim the resurrection of Jesus and stretch well into the future. These new faith genealogies will be lists of men and women who hear the story of Jesus and live lives of faith. The continuing story of faith will not be passed along in a single family; it will be passed along to all of the nations. The Gospel of Matthew ends, then, with an implied list of names, stretching from the disciples to countless people today.

A "New" Commission

Why does the gospel end with a new commission? Jesus had already called his disciples. He had already given them authority. Why doesn't Jesus say, "Go and do what you were told to do all along!" This may sound like an odd question. But, I do not mean for it to sound irreverent. Why does Jesus end his time with his disciples by re-calling them, re-commissioning them?

Simply stated, the new commission is based upon their experience with the risen Jesus, the resurrected Jesus. It is only in the resurrection that the disciples experience God's ultimate promise that from expected death comes unexpected new life. This is a new message and, therefore, there must be a new commission. The disciples are now able to bring the promise of new life to all the world in a way that they could not have previously done. The message of Jesus is incomplete without the proclamation of his crucifixion and of his resurrection. The faith that is to be passed along depends upon the proclamation of the empty tomb.

It is not enough for the disciples to base their ministry on the Beatitudes alone. It is true that they will continue to relabel those who have been cast out. They will invite the outsider in. They will bless those that the world sees as shameful. But, this is not enough. It is not enough to be agents of healing. It is true that they will work to heal the social wounds brought about by alienation and rejection. But, this is not enough. It is not enough to continue to teach as Jesus taught. It is true that the disciples will continue to examine what God's laws might mean for the life of the faithful. They will ask, "How should we strive to live in community; to live in healthy relationships with God and with one another?" But, this is not enough. The disciples must incorporate their experience with the risen Jesus into all they do and all they say.

This new commission, based upon their experience with the risen Jesus, insures that their message cannot be reduced to the words and deeds of Jesus alone. The Jesus story is incomplete without the proclamation of the resurrection. In modern terms, we might say that the new commission insures Jesus cannot be reduced to simply being viewed as a good teacher or an example of morality. The words and deeds of Jesus were important, and are important. But, they are also incomplete with the proclamation of the resurrection. Jesus had to re-commission the disciples because they were commissioned with a different message, a message that includes the promise of the resurrection, the ultimate example of the promise of unexpected new life.

Some Doubted

Why does the Gospel of Matthew include the detail that some of the disciples doubted? This detail is not explained. We are not told anything specific, just that some doubted. The inclusion of this doubt may seem to be at odds with the rest of this story. The disciples hear the good news; they gather together with the risen Jesus on a mountain in Galilee; they worship. Wouldn't the story have a better flow if it went from their worship straight into the words of commission? The story is clearly ending on the highest of notes. The good news of the resurrection proves that the crucifixion, the death of Jesus, was not the end of the story. The gathering of the disciples works to negate their denial and abandonment of Jesus. The worship of the disciples wipes out the mockery of those who watched him die. This is a story of dramatic reversals. So, why include the detail that some doubted?

Our author never shies away from the reality of struggle, suffering, doubt, and death. And, it is important that this reality is included here. In the genealogy of Jesus, the author included stories where the family and its faith faced expected death. The birth story of Jesus was told in the context of a probable honor killing. Death loomed large during Joseph's dilemma. While Joseph, Mary, and the baby Jesus escaped to Egypt, Herod killed all children two and under around the city of Bethlehem.

When Jesus heard about the death of John the Baptist, he went away to be alone, to grieve. The author of the Gospel of Matthew could have told the story of Jesus without including stories of struggle, suffering, doubt, and death. But, this is not the story that we are told. We are given a gospel that takes seriously the reality of death. A story about faith is only half told if it is told without doubt.

By including the note that some doubted, the author is acknowledging that even the experience of the resurrected Jesus does not eliminate the very natural, very human, feeling of doubt. By including this detail, the author is telling all readers of the gospel that even those that experienced the risen Jesus had questions and doubt. Moreover, the author shows that the doubt of the disciples does not keep them from being called, from being commissioned. Doubt does not prevent the disciples from engaging in a life of ministry. In other words, doubt is not incompatible with ministry. In fact, the opposite is true. Armed with both faith and doubt, the disciples are sent out to make disciples of all nations. The doubt of the disciples, then, can be good news for readers of Matthew.

Unexpected New Life for All Nations

Throughout the Gospel of Matthew, Jesus promises new life to members of "all the nations." There was a sense of very strong group orientation in the ancient world of the New Testament. People were concerned with members of their own family, their own social group, and were often quite hostile to others. It was a world where you were either in or you were out. Group boundaries were clear, well defined, and upheld with great rigor. In this context, Jesus' words and actions display radical inclusivity.

On one occasion when Jesus entered Capernaum, a centurion came to him. The man appealed to Jesus, saying, "Lord, my servant is lying at home paralyzed, in terrible distress" (8:5–6). Jesus immediately responded, "I will come and cure him" (8:7). We experience the healing and curing touch of Jesus throughout this gospel. But in this case, we are reminded that Jesus was not concerned with typical group boundaries, group barriers. In fact, he was concerned with tearing down such boundaries. The centurion was a Roman and would have been regarded as an enemy to all those in first-century Galilee. We might assume that even the disciples of Jesus were surprised at this turn of events. Jesus is healing the servant of a Roman centurion? If he will do this, where will he draw the line?

On another occasion, a group of Pharisees attempted to challenge Jesus. Hearing that he had silenced the Sadducees, one of them asked, "Teacher, which commandment is the greatest" (22:34–36)? Jesus answered, "You shall love the Lord your God with all your heart, and with all your soul, and with all your mind.' This is the greatest and first commandment. And a second is like it: 'You shall love your neighbor as yourself'" (37–39). Perhaps modern readers have heard the commandment to "love your neighbor" so many times that it has lost some of its impact. Perhaps we do not fully grasp what this might have meant in its original cultural context. Either way, the words do not seem to be radically inclusive. However, Jesus is commanding that we love one another without paying attention to traditional boundaries. He is instructing us to love beyond the safe confines of our own families and our own social groups. We are to reach out with our love.

Again and again, Jesus shows complete disregard for traditional boundaries in his teaching and healing, in his displays of love and forgiveness. Now, in this final commission to his disciples, he instructs them to make disciples of all nations. The eleven are not to see the world in terms of who is in and who is out. Rather, they are to look at everyone as worthy of the good news. The disciples are to bring the promise of unexpected new life to all the nations.

Unexpected New Life in Baptism

In his final words to his disciples, Jesus explains that they are to "baptize in the name of the Father and of the Son and of the Holy Spirit" (28:19). The gospel does not include any other instructions concerning baptism. The disciples are not told at what age a person is to be baptized. They are not told if the one being baptized is to be fully immersed in water or if a sprinkling is sufficient. They are only told to use what we call Trinitarian language.

The *Didache*, a Christian handbook written shortly after the Gospel of Matthew, provides some further insight into how early Christ-followers understood and performed baptisms. "Concerning baptism, baptize in this way: Having first rehearsed all these things, 'baptize in the name of the Father and of the Son and of the Holy Spirit,' in running water; but if you have no running water, baptize in other water, and if you cannot in cold, then in warm. But if you have neither, pour water three times on the head 'in the name of the Father, Son and Holy Spirit'" (*Didache* 7:1–3).

This section from the *Didache* ("Teaching") is telling in its openness to a wide variety of baptismal styles. The type of water, the amount of water, and the specific setting is not as important as the promise that accompanies the act. With water and words, the one being baptized is brought into the Christian community. But more than this, the promise that from expected death comes unexpected new life is proclaimed in a most tangible manner. There is a promise that accompanies the water, the promise of new life. In baptism, the victory that Jesus experienced over the grave is promised to the newly baptized. Death does not have the final say. Death does not win. Rather, the promise of unexpected new life is a gift of grace that is experienced in the waters of baptism. In this final great commission, the disciples are instructed to bring this promise of new life to all the nations. The disciples are to baptize everyone in the name of the Father and of the Son and of the Holy Spirit.

Teaching the Message of Unexpected New Life

The disciples are also to teach people to "obey everything that Jesus has commanded" (28:20). Throughout his ministry, Jesus offered many commandments. For example, during his Sermon on the Mount, he gave instructions, or commandments, regarding love for enemies. Jesus explained, "You have heard that it was said, 'You shall love your neighbor and hate your enemy.' But I say to you, Love your enemies and pray for those who persecute you, so that you may be children of your Father in heaven; for he makes his sun rise on the evil and on the good, and sends rain on the righteous and on the unrighteous. For if you love those who love you, what reward do you have? Do not even the tax collectors do the same? And if you greet only your brothers and sisters, what more are you doing than others? Do not even the Gentiles do the same? Be perfect, therefore, as your heavenly Father is perfect" (5:43–48).

The call to love one's enemy is a helpful example of the nature of Jesus' commandments. When Jesus presents a commandment, it follows three rules. First, each commandment is based upon the need to be loving and gracious in our dealings with God and with one another. Second, the commandments emphasize the need to look past traditional boundaries, seeing the hurt and the needs of others regardless of their social standing. Third, Jesus' commandments bring the promise of new life to those facing situations of death.

We can test these three rules when reading the words of Jesus. For example, he commands, "in everything do to others as you would have them do to you; for this is the law and the prophets" (7:12). In other words, this instruction is a summary of everything that has come before it. This Great Commandment, this Golden Rule, emphasizes the need for mutual love and shared expressions of grace. Furthermore, it asks us to look past the cultural rules that might typically inform our behavior. Instead we are to ask, "How do I want to be treated? How do I want to be treated by my friends and family? How do I want to be treated by strangers and even enemies?" If we wish to be the recipients of love and grace, we must be agents of love and grace. Finally, if this practice is followed, if this command is kept, if we are agents of love and grace, we will also be agents of new life.

Jesus commissions his disciples with these words: "make disciples of all nations . . . teaching them to obey everything that I have commanded you." Here Jesus is again extending the call for love and grace to be the rule in every relationship. He is commanding the disciples and members of all the nations to extend this love and grace beyond traditional boundaries. And, in so doing, he is promising the experience of unexpected new life.

Conclusion

It is with words of tremendous hope and promise that Jesus concludes his new commission: "And remember, I am with you always to the end of the age" (28:20). These words conclude Jesus' teaching and are the final words of our gospel. With them, Jesus is proclaiming that the promise of unexpected new life is a promise that is eternal. From the first names in the genealogy to the last words spoken by Jesus, we witness the promise that from expected death comes unexpected new life. Through the actions of Tamar, we experience the promise of unexpected new life. Through the actions of Rahab, Ruth, and Bathsheba, we experience the promise of unexpected new life. In the birth story of Jesus and in Joseph's dilemma, we anticipate the killing of Mary. In fact, from the womb to the tomb, we experience death. But, from the womb to the tomb, we also experience the promise of unexpected new life. In the birth, life, ministry, death, and resurrection of Jesus, the Gospel of Matthew proclaims the message that from expected death comes unexpected new life.

Bibliography

Abu-Hilal, Ahmad. "Arab and North-American Social Attitudes: Some Cross-Cultural Comparisons." *Mankind Quarterly* 22 (1982) 193–207.

Abu-Lughod, Leila. *Veiled Sentiments: Honor and Piety in a Bedouin Society.* Berkeley: University of California Press, 1986.

Abu-Odeh, Lama. "Crimes of Honour and the Construction of Gender in Arab Society." In *Feminism and Islam: Legal and Literary Perspectives*, 141–194. Edited by Mai Yamani. New York: New York University Press, 1996.

Abu-Toameh, Khaled. "Report Says Palestinian 'Honor Killings' are Increasing." *Jerusalem Post*, May 30, 2007, News 3.

Afkhami, Mahnaz. *Faith & Freedom: Women's Human Rights in the Muslim World.* Syracuse, NY: Syracuse University Press, 1995.

BBC News. "One in 10 'Backs Honour Killings.'" September 4, 2006, http://news.bbc. co.uk/2/hi/uk_news/5311244.stm.

Ahmed, Leila. *Women and Gender in Islam: Historical Roots of a Modern Debate.* New Haven, CT: Yale University Press, 1992.

Albright, W. F. and C. S. Mann. *Matthew.* AB 26. New York: Doubleday, 1971.

Al-Fanar (Palestinian feminist organization). "Developments in the Struggle against the Murder of Women against the Background of So-Called Family Honor." *Women Against Fundamentalism Journal* 6 (1995) 37–41.

Al-Khayyat, Sana. *Honour and Shame: Women in Modern Iraq.* London: Saqi Books, 1990.

Allison, Dale C. "Divorce, Celibacy and Joseph (Matthew 1.18–25 and 19.1–12)." *Journal for the Study of the New Testament* 49 (1993) 3–10.

Al-Malaika, Nazik. *A Tranquil Moment of a Wave.* Beirut, 1957.

Anderson, Janice Capel. "Mary's Difference: Gender and Patriarchy in the Birth Narratives." *Journal of Religion* 67.2 (1987) 183–202.

Antonelli, Alessandra. "Crimes Not Stories." *Palestine Report*, 22 May 1998, 13, 16.

Antoun, Richard T. *Arab Village: A Social Structural Study of a Trans-Jordanian Peasant Community.* Bloomington: Indiana University Press, 1972.

Araji, S. K., and J. Carlson. "Family Violence Including Crimes of Honor in Jordan." *Violence Against Women* 7.5 (2001) 586–621.

Argyle, A. W. *The Gospel according to Matthew.* Cambridge, MA: Cambridge University Press, 1963.

Aune, David E., editor. *Greco-Roman Literature and the New Testament: Selected Forms and Genres.* SBL Sources for Biblical Study 21. Atlanta: Scholars, 1988.

———. *The New Testament in Its Literary Environment*. Cambridge, MA: James Clarke, 1988.

Bailey, James L., and Lyle D. Vander Broek. *Literary Forms in the New Testament: A Handbook*. Louisville: Westminster John Knox, 1992.

Baker, N. V., P. R. Gregware, and M. A. Cassidy. "Family Killing Fields: Honor Rationales in the Murder of Women." *Violence Against Women* 5.2 (1999) 164–84.

Barton, Carlin A. *Roman Honor: The Fire in the Bones*. Berkeley: University of California Press, 2001.

Beare, Francis Wright. *The Gospel according to Matthew: A Commentary*. Oxford: Blackwell, 1981.

Benson, G. P. "Virgin Birth, Virgin Conception." *Expository Times* 98.5 (1987) 139–40.

Beyer, Lisa, and Jo LeGood. "The Price of Honor: Jordanians Are Fighting a Brutal Arab Tradition—The Murder of Women for Alleged Sexual Impropriety." *Time* 153.2 (1999) 55.

Bilefsky, Dan. "How to Avoid Honor Killing in Turkey? Honor Suicide." *New York Times*, 16 July 2006, 1.3.

Bird, Steve. "'My Family Said I Had Destroyed Their Name.'" *The Times*, 13 June 2007, News 15.

———. "'Honour' Killing Used to Threaten Others." *The Times*, 13 June 2007, News 15.

Blomberg, Craig, L. "The Liberation of Illegitimacy: Women and Rulers in Matthew 1–2." *Biblical Theology Bulletin* 21 (1991) 145–50.

Boring, M. Eugene. *Matthew*. NIB 8. Nashville: Abingdon, 1995.

Bornkamm, Günther et al. *Tradition and Interpretation in Matthew*. Philadelphia: Westminster, 1963.

Boslooper, Thomas. "Jesus' Virgin Birth and Non-Christian 'Parallels.'" *Religion in Life* 26.1 (Winter 1956–57) 87–97.

———. *The Virgin Birth*. Philadelphia: Westminster, 1962.

Bostock, Gerald. "Virgin Birth or Human Conception?" *Expository Times* 97.9 (1986) 260–63.

Bourdieu, Pierre. "The Sentiment of Honour in Kabyle Society." In *Honour and Shame*, edited by J. G. Peristiany, 191–241. London: Weidenfeld and Nicholson, 1966.

Bourke, Myles M. Review of *The Birth of the Messiah: A Commentary on the Infancy Narratives in Matthew and Luke*, by Raymond E. Brown. *Catholic Biblical Quarterly* 40 (1978) 120–24.

Bowen, Donna Lee, and Evelyn A. Early. *Everyday Life in the Muslim Middle East*. 2nd ed. Bloomington: Indiana University Press, 2002.

Brandes, Stanley. "Reflections on Honor and Shame in the Mediterranean." In *Honor and Shame in the Unity of the Mediterranean*, 121–34. Edited by David D. Gilmore. Washington, DC: American Anthropological Association, 1987.

Brayford, Susan A. "To Shame or Not to Shame: Sexuality in the Mediterranean Diaspora." *Semeia* 87 (1999) 163–76.

Brooks, Geraldine. *Nine Parts of Desire: The Hidden World of Islamic Women*. New York: Anchor, 1995.

Brown, Raymond E. "The Problem of the Virginal Conception of Jesus." *Theological Studies* 33.1 (1972) 3–34.

———. *The Virginal Conception and Bodily Resurrection of Jesus*. New York: Paulist, 1973.

———. "Gospel Infancy Narrative Research from 1976 to 1986: Part 1 (Matthew)." *Catholic Biblical Quarterly* 48.3 (July 1986) 468–83.

————. *The Birth of the Messiah: A Commentary on the Infancy Narratives in Matthew and Luke*. New York: Doubleday, 1993.

Buchanan, George Wesley. *The Gospel of Matthew*. Mellen Biblical Commentary 1.1. Lewiston, NY: Mellen Biblical, 1996.

Burn, Shawn Meghan. *Women Across Cultures: A Global Perspective*. 2nd ed. New York: McGraw-Hill, 2005.

Burridge, Richard A. *What Are the Gospels?: A Comparison with Graeco-Roman Biography*. 2nd ed. Dearborn, MI: Dove, 2004.

Calkins, Arthur Burton. "The Justice of Joseph Revisited." In *Kecharitōmenē*, 165–77. Paris: Desclée, 1990.

Campbell, J. K. *Honour, Family, and Patronage: A Study of Institutions and Moral Values in a Greek Mountain Community*. New York: Oxford University Press, 1974.

Campenhausen, Hans Freiherr von. *The Virgin Birth in the Theology of the Ancient Church*. London: SCM, 1964.

Caner, Ergun Mehmet. *Voices behind the Veil: The World of Islam through the Eyes of Women*. Grand Rapids: Kregel, 2004.

Carnell, Edward John. "The Virgin Birth of Christ." *Christianity Today*, 7 December 1959, 9–10.

Carr, A. *The Gospel according to St. Matthew*. Cambridge: Cambridge University Press, 1890.

Carter, Warren. *Matthew and the Margins: A Sociopolitical and Religious Reading*. Maryknoll: Orbis, 2000.

Cave, C.H. "St. Matthew's Infancy Narrative." *New Testament Studies* 9 (1962–63) 382–90.

Chance, John K. "The Anthropology of Honor and Shame: Culture, Values, and Practice." *Semeia* 68 (1996) 139–51.

Charlesworth, James H., editor. *The Old Testament Pseudepigraph*. Vol. 2. Garden City, NY: Doubleday, 1985.

Clark, Alan C. "The Virgin Birth: A Theological Reappraisal." *Theological Studies* 34.4 (1973) 576–93.

Combs-Schilling, M. E. *Sacred Performances: Islam, Sexuality and Sacrifice*. New York: Columbia University Press, 1989.

Coulson, Noel J. "Regulation of Sexual Behavior under Traditional Islamic Law." In *Society and the Sexes in Medieval Islam*, 63–68. Edited by Afaf Lutfi Al-Sayyid Marsot. Malibu, CA: Undena, 1977.

Cox, G. E. P. *The Gospel sccording to Saint Matthew: Introduction and Commentary*. London: SCM, 1958.

Cranfield, C. E. B. "Some Reflections on the Subject of the Virgin Birth." *Scottish Journal of Theology* 41.2 (1988) 177–89.

Saywell, Shelley. writer and director. *Crimes of Honor*. New York: First Run/Icarus Films, 1998.

Crouch, James E. "How Early Christians Viewed the Birth of Jesus." *Bible Review* 7 (1991) 34–38.

Daniélou, Jean. *The Infancy Narratives*. New York: Herder, 1968.

Davies, Margaret. *Matthew*. Sheffield: JSOT Press, 1993.

Davis, J. *People of the Mediterranean: An Essay in Comparative Social Anthropology*. London: Routledge & Kegan Paul, 1977.

Delaney, Carol. "Seeds of Honor, Fields of Shame." In *Honor and Shame in the Unity of the Mediterranean*, 35–48. Edited by David D. Gilmore. Washington, DC: American Anthropological Association, 1987.

Didache. In *The Apostolic Fathers*, vol. 1. With translation by Kirsopp Lake. LCL. Cambridge: Harvard University Press, 1985.

Dihle, Albrecht. *Greek and Latin Literature of the Roman Empire: From Augustus to Justinian*. 3rd ed. London: Routledge, 1994.

Dodd, Peter C. "Family Honor and the Forces of Change in Arab Society." *International Journal of Middle East Studies* 4.1 (1973) 40–54.

Dodds, Paisley. "Father Guilty in 'Honor Killing.'" *Chicago Tribune*, 12 June 2007, World 12.

Doumanis, Mariella. *Mothering in Greece: From Collectivism to Individualism*. London: Academic Press, 1983.

Down, M.J. "The Matthean Birth Narratives: Matthew 1:18–2:23." *Expository Times* 90 (1978–79) 51–52.

Dunne, Bruce. "Power and Sexuality in the Middle East." *Middle East Report* 28.1 (1998) 8–11.

Duzkan, A., and F. Kocali. "An Honor Killing: She Fled, Her Throat Was Cut." In *Women and Sexuality in Muslim Societies*, edited by Pinar Ilkkaracan. Istanbul: Women for Women's Human Rights, 2000.

Edwards, Douglas. *The Virgin Birth in History and Faith*. London: Faber, 1943.

Edwards, Richard A. *Matthew's Story of Jesus*. Philadelphia: Fortress, 1985.

Eggers, Wilhelm. *How to Read the New Testament: An Introduction to Linguistic and Historical-Critical Methodology*. Peabody, MA: Hendrickson, 1996.

Elass, Rasha. "'Honor' Killing Spurs Outcry in Syria." *Christian Science Monitor*, 24 February 2007, World 7.

Elliott, J. K. *The Apocryphal Jesus: Legends of the Early Church*. Oxford: Oxford University Press, 1996.

———, editor. *The Apocryphal New Testament: A Collection of Apocryphal Christian Literature in an English Translation Based on M. R. James*. New York: Oxford, 2005.

———. *A Synopsis of the Apocryphal Nativity and Infancy Narratives*. Leiden: Brill, 2006.

El Saadawi, Nawal. *The Hidden Face of Eve: Women in the Arab World*. Translated and edited by Sherif Hetata. Boston: Beacon, 1982.

Emery, James. "Reputation Is Everything: Honor Killings among the Palestinians." *The World and I*, May 2003, 182–91.

Erdman, Charles, R. *The Gospel of Matthew*. Philadelphia: Westminster, 1948.

Esler, Philip F. *The First Christians in the Social Worlds: Social-Scientific Approaches to New Testament Interpretation*. London: Routledge, 1994.

Evans, Martin. "Killed by Her Own Family for 'Honour.'" *The Express*, 15 July 2006, News 16.

Fenton, J. C. *Saint Matthew*. Westminster Pelican Commentaries. Philadelphia: Westminster, 1963.

Filson, Floyd V. *A Commentary on the Gospel according to St. Matthew*. London: A. & C. Black, 1960.

Finkelstein, J. J. "Sex Offenses in Sumerian Laws." *Journal of the American Oriental Society* 86 (1966) 362–63.

Fitzmyer, Joseph A. "The Virginal Conception of Jesus in the New Testament." *Theological Studies* 34.4 (1973) 541–75.

France, R. T. "Scripture, Tradition and History in the Infancy Narratives of Matthew." In *Gospel Perspectives*, vol. 2, *Studies of History and Tradition in the Four Gospels*, 239–66. Edited by R. T. France and David Wenham. Sheffield: JSOT Press, 1981.

———. *The Gospel according to Matthew: An Introduction and Commentary*. NICNT. Grand Rapids: Eerdmans, 1985.

Franchetti, Mark. "Iraqi Women Die in 'Honour' Murders." *Sunday Times*, 28 September 2003, News 25.

Freed, Edwin D. "The Women in Matthew's Genealogy." *Journal for the Study of the New Testament* 29 (1987) 3–19.

———. *The Stories of Jesus' Birth: A Critical Introduction*. Sheffield: Sheffield Academic, 2001.

Gairola, Rahul. "Burning with Shame: Desire and South Asian Patriarchy, from Gayatri Spivak's 'Can the Subaltern Speak?' to Deepa Mehta's *Fire*." *Comparative Literature* 54.4 (2002) 307–24.

Garland, David E. *Reading Matthew: A Literary and Theological Commentary on the First Gospel*. London: SPCK, 1993.

Gilmore, David D., editor. *Honor and Shame and the Unity of the Mediterranean*. Washington, DC: American Anthropological Association, 1987.

———. "Introduction: The Shame of Dishonor." In *Honor and Shame in the Unity of the Mediterranean*, 2–21. Edited by David D. Gilmore. Washington, DC: American Anthropological Association, 1987.

Goldstein, Matthew A. "The Biological Roots of Heat-of-Passion Crimes and Honor Killings." *Politics and the Life Sciences* 21.2 (2002) 28–37.

Goodenough, Patrick. "Blood and Honor." *Middle East Digest*, February 1995, 1–5.

Goodwin, Jan. *Price of Honour: Muslim Women Lift the Veil of Silence on the Islamic World*. London: Warner, 1995.

Green, F. W. *The Gospel according to Saint Matthew*. Oxford: Clarendon, 1936.

Green, H. Benedict. *The Gospel according to Matthew*. Oxford: Oxford University Press, 1975.

Gregg, Gary S. *The Middle East: A Cultural Psychology*. Oxford: Oxford University Press, 2005.

Gundy, Robert H. *Matthew: A Commentary on His Literary and Theological Art*. Grand Rapids: Eerdmans, 1982.

———. *Matthew: A Commentary on His Handbook for a Mixed Church under Persecution*. Grand Rapids: Eerdmans, 1994.

Haeri, S. "The Politics of Dishonor: Rape and Power in Pakistan." In *Faith and Freedom: Women's Human Rights in the Muslim World*, 167–74. Edited by M. Afkhami. Syracuse, NY: Syracuse University Press, 1995.

Hagner, Donald A. *Matthew 1–13*. WBC 33A. Dallas: Word, 1993.

Hamzeh-Muhaisen, Muna. "Violence against Women: Who Will Stop the Men?" *Palestine Report*, 10 October 1997, 4–5.

Hanson, K. C. and Douglas E. Oakman. *Palestine in the Time of Jesus: Social Structures and Social Conflicts*. Minneapolis: Fortress, 2002.

Hare, Douglas R. A. *Matthew*. Interpretation. Louisville: John Knox, 1993.

Harrington, Daniel J. *The Gospel of Matthew*. Sacra Pagina 1. Collegeville, MN: Liturgical, 1991.

Hasan, Manar. "The Politics of Honor: Patriarchy, the State and the Murder of Women in the Name of Family Honor." *Journal of Israeli History* 21 (2002) 1–37.

Hawley, Richard, and Barbara Levick, editors. *Women in Antiquity: New Assessments.* London: Routledge, 1995.

Hegland, Mary Elaine. "Gender and Islam: Women's Accommodating Resistance." In *Social History of Women and Gender in the Modern Middle East*, 186–97. Edited by Margaret L. Meriwether and Judith E. Tucker. Boulder, CO: Westview, 1999.

Hendrickx, Herman. *The Infancy Narratives.* London: G. Chapman, 1984.

Hill, David. *The Gospel of Matthew.* London: Oliphants, 1978.

Hock, Ronald. F. *The Infancy Gospels of James and Thomas: With Introductions, Notes, and Original Text Featuring the New Scholars Version Translation.* Santa Rosa, CA: Polebridge, 1995.

————. *The Life of Mary and Birth of Jesus.* Berkeley, CA: Ulysses, 1997

Davie, Michael, Sean Fine, and Andy Gray. "Honor Killings." *National Geographic Television.* 2001–2002.

Horsley, Richard A. *The Liberation of Christmas: The Infancy Narratives in Social Context.* New York: Continuum, 1989.

Ilkkaracan, Pinar. "Exploring the Context of Women's Sexuality in Eastern Turkey." *Reproductive Health Matters* 6.12 (1998) 66–75.

International Orthodox Christian Charities. "A Glimmer of Hope: Qellem Wollega Podoconiosis Prevention and Control Program Presentation." August 2009.

Instone-Brewer, David. *Divorce and Remarriage in the Bible: The Social and Literary Context.* Grand Rapids: Eerdmans, 2002.

Jaber, Hala. "'Honour' Killings Grow as Girl, 17, Stoned to Death." *The Times*, 4 November 2007, News 25.

Jehl, Douglas. "For Shame: A Special Report. Arab Honor's Price: A Woman's Blood." *New York Times*, 20 June 1999, 1.1.

Jones, Ivor H. *The Gospel of Matthew.* London: Epworth, 1994.

Josephus. *Jewish Antiquities: Books 7–8.* Translated by Ralph Marcus. LCL. Cambridge, MA: Harvard University Press, 1934.

————. *Jewish Antiquities: Books 16–17.* Translated by Ralph Marcus and Allen Wikgren. LCL. Cambridge, MA: Harvard University Press, 1963.

————. *The Jewish War: Books 1–11.* Translated by H. St. J. Thackeray. LCL. Cambridge, MA: Harvard University Press, 1997.

Judd, Terri. "Stabbed to Death as Her Family Watched . . . for Honour." *The Independent*, 15 July 2006, News 18.

Juschka, Amy. "The Binary Hoax: Honour Killings in the Middle East or a Massacre in Montreal—Recognizing Expressions of Patriarchy." *Briarpatch* 34.2 (2005) 21–23.

Keddie, Nikki R. *Women in the Middle East: Past and Present.* Princeton, NJ: Princeton University Press, 2007.

Keener, Craig S. *A Commentary on the Gospel of Matthew.* Grand Rapids: Eerdmans, 1999.

Kent, Paul. "Young Love . . . Two Ancient Religions . . . s Women Dying in a Pool of her Own Blood sfter a Public Stoning: The Price Dua'a Paid." *Hobart Mercury*, 24 May 2007, 9.

Khaki, M. Aslam. *Honour, Killings in Pakistan & Islamic View.* Islamabad: Insaaf Welfare Trust, 2004.

Khan, Sheema. "Uprooting Age-Old Customs from Within: Muslims Must Speak Out against Such Practices as Honor Killings and Female Genital Mutilation." *Globe and Mail*, 9 October 2007, A21.

Kim, E. *Ten Thousand Sorrows.* Canada: Doubleday, 2000.

Kingsbury, Jack Dean. *Matthew: Structure, Christology, Kingdom.* Philadelphia: Fortress, 1975.

Korvarik, Chiara Angela. *Interviews with Muslim Women of Pakistan.* Minneapolis: Syren, 2004.

Kress, Rory. "Gazans Suspect Murder of Sisters Was Honor Killing." *Jerusalem Post,* 25 July 2007, News 6.

Kulwicki, A. D. "The Practice of Honor Crimes: A Glimpse of Domestic Violence in the Arab World." *Issues In Mental Health Nursing* 23.1 (2002) 77–87.

Laurentin, René. *The Truth of Christmas: Beyond the Myths.* Translated by Micahel J. Wrenn. Petersham: St. Bede's. 1986.

Leaney, A. R. C. "Birth Narratives in St Luke and St Matthew." *New Testament Studies* 8 (1962) 158–66.

Lefkowitz, Mary R., and Maureen B. Fant. *Women's Life in Greece and Rome: A Source Book in Translation.* 3rd ed. Baltimore: Johns Hopkins University Press, 2005.

Levine, Amy-Jill, and Marianne Blickenstaff, editors. *A Feminist Companion to Matthew.* Sheffield: Sheffield Academic, 2001.

Levinson, Bernard M. *Deuteronomy and the Hermeneutics of Legal Innovation.* Oxford: Oxford University Press, 2002.

Logmans, A., A. Verhoeff, R. Bol Raap, R. Creighton, and M. van Lent. "Ethical Dilemma: Should Doctors Reconstruct the Vaginal Introitus of Adolescent Girls to Mimic the Virginal State? (Who Wants the Procedure and Why)." *British Medical Journal* 316 (1998) 459–60.

Loudon, Bruce. "Pakistan Police Fail as 'Honour Killings Soar.'" *Weekend Australian,* 10 February 2007. World 16.

———. "Pakistan's 'Honour Killers' Go Free." *Weekend Australian,* 10 February 2007, World 16.

Khanum, Saeeda, director. *Love, Honor, and Disobey.* Faction Films, 2005.

Lüdemann, Gerd. *Virgin Birth?: The Real Story of Mary and Her Son Jesus.* Translated by John Bowden. London: SCM, 1998.

Luz, Ulrich. *Matthew 1–7.* Translated by Wilhelm C. Linss. Edinburgh: T. & T. Clark, 1990.

Machen, J. Gresham. *The Virgin Birth of Christ.* New York: Harper, 1930.

Malina, Bruce J. *The New Testament World: Insights from Cultural Anthropology.* 3rd ed. Louisville: Westminster John Knox, 2001.

Malina, Bruce J., and Richard L. Rohrbaugh. *Social-Science Commentary on the Synoptic Gospels.* Minneapolis: Fortress, 1992.

Marohl, Matthew J. *Joseph's Dilemma: "Honor Killing" in the Birth Narrative of Matthew.* Eugene, OR: Cascade, 2008.

Massaux, E. *The Influence of the Gospel of Matthew on Christian Literature before Saint Irenaeus.* 2 vols. Translated by N. Belval and S. Hecht. New Gospel Studies 5. Atlanta: Mercer University Press, 1990.

Matthews, Victor H. "Honor and Shame in Gender-Related Legal Situations in the Hebrew Bible." In *Gender and Law in the Hebrew Bible and the Ancient Near East,* 97–112. Edited by Victor H. Matthews, Bernard M. Levinson, and Tikva Frymer-Kensky. JSOTSup 262. Sheffield: Sheffield Academic, 1998.

McGreal, Chris. "Murdered in the Name of Family Honour: Chris McGreal Reports from Ramallah on a Rise in Killings of Palestinian Women." *The Guardian,* 1 July 2005, 18.

McKeating, Henry. "Sanctions against Adultery in Ancient Israelite Society, with Some Reflections on Methodology in the Study of Old Testament Ethics." *Journal for the Study of the Old Testament* 11 (1979) 57–63.

Mernissi, Fatima. "Virginity and Patriarchy." *Women's Studies International Forum* 5.2 (1982) 183–91.

Metzger, Bruce M. *An Introduction to The Apocrypha.* New York: Oxford University Press, 1969.

Micklem, Philip A. *St Matthew.* London: Methuen, 1917.

Migne, Jacques Paul, editor. *Patrologiae Cursus Completus.* Series Graeca. 166 volumes. Paris: Migne, 1857–1886.

Miller, Karyn, and Tom Harper. "'Honour Killings' Increasing in Britain as Women Stand Up for their Rights." *The Sunday Telegraph,* 16 July 2006. News 10.

Minear, Paul S. *Matthew: The Teacher's Gospel.* London: Darton, Longman, and Todd, 1982.

M'Neile, Alan Hugh. *The Gospel according to St. Mathew.* London: MacMillan, 1915.

Moghaizel, Laure. "The Arab and Mediterranean World: Legislation Toward Crimes of Honor." In *Empowerment and the Law: Strategies of Third World Women,* edited by Margaret Schuler, 174–80. Washington, DC: OEF International, 1986.

Mojab, Shahrzad. "'Honor Killing': Culture, Politics, and Theory." *Middle East Women's Studies Review* 17.1–2 (2002) 1–7.

Mojab, Shahrzad, and Amir Hassanpour. "Thoughts on the Struggle against 'Honor Killing.'" *International Journal of Kurdish Studies* 16.1–2 (2002) 83–97.

———. "The Politics and Culture of 'Honor Killing': The Murder of Fadime Şahindal." *Pakistan Journal of Women's Studies: Alam-e-Niswan* 9.1 (2002) 57–77.

Morris, Leon. *The Gospel according to Matthew.* Grand Rapids: Eerdmans, 1992.

Mosquera, Patricia M. Rodriguez, et al. "Honor in the Mediterranean and Northern Europe." *Journal of Cross-Cultural Psychology* 33.1 (2002) 16–36.

Mounce, Robert H. *Matthew.* NIBC. Peabody, MA: Hendrickson, 1991.

Moxness, Halvor. "Honor and Shame." In *The Social Sciences and New Testament Interpretation,* 19–40. Edited by Richard Rohrbaugh. Peabody, MA: Hendrickson, 1996.

———. *Putting Jesus in His Place: A Radical Vision of Household and Kingdom.* Louisville: Westminster John Knox, 2003.

Mulholland, M. Robert, Jr. "The Infancy Narratives in Matthew and Luke: Of History, Theology, and Literature." *Biblical Archaeology Review* 7.2 (1981) 46–59.

Naber, Nadine. "Teaching about Honor Killings and Other Sensitive Topics in Middle East Studies." *Middle East Women's Study Review* 15.1–2 (2002) 20–21.

Narayan, Uma. "Cross-Cultural Connections, Border-Crossings, and 'Death by Culture:' Thinking about Dowry-Murders in India and Domestic-Violence Murders in the United States." In *Dislocating Cultures: Identities, Traditions, and Third World Feminism,* 81–117. New York: Routledge, 1997.

Neighbour, Margaret. "Honour Killing Plea to Pakistan's Leader." *The Scotsman,* 21 September 2005, 25.

Newell, Katherine S., et al. *Discrimination against the Girl Child: Female Infanticide, Female Genital Cutting, and Honor Killing.* Washington, DC: Youth Advocate Program International, 2000.

Neyrey, Jerome H. *Honor and Shame in the Gospel of Matthew.* Louisville: Westminster John Knox, 1998.

Nickerson, Colin. "For Muslim Women, A Deadly Defiance: 'Honor Killings' on Rise in Europe." *The Boston Globe*, 16 January 2006, Nationan/Foreign, A1.

Nolland, John. "The Four (Five) Women and Other Annotations in Matthew's Genealogy." *New Testament Studies* 43 (1997) 527–39.

Nowell, Irene. "Jesus' Great-Grandmothers: Matthew's Four and More." *Catholic Biblical Quarterly* 70.1 (January 2008) 1–15.

Rikskringkasting, Norsk. *Our Honour, His Glory*. Sveriges Television. New York: Filmakers Library, 1997.

Palestinian Human Rights Monitoring Group. "Honor Killing: Killing Women on the Basis of Family Honor." *The Monitor* 6.4 (Aug 2002).

Palestinian Ma'an News Agency. "Palesinian Agency says 2006 'Blookiest Year' for 'Honour Killings.'" Translated by BBC Monitoring Middle East. December 4, 2006.

Parrot, Andrea and Nina Cummings. *Forsaken Females: The Global Brutalization of Women*. Lanham: Rowman & Littlefield, 2006.

Patte, Daniel. *The Gospel according to Matthew: A Structural Commentary on Matthew's Faith*. Philadelphia: Fortress, 1987.

Peake, Arthur S. "The Supernatural Birth of Jesus." *Methodist Quarterly Review* 73.4 (1924) 579–91.

Peristiany, J. G., editor. *Honour and Grace in Anthropology*. Cambridge, MA: Cambridge University Press, 1992.

Peristiany, J. G., editor. *Honour and Shame: The Values of Mediterranean Society*. London: Weidenfeld and Nicholson, 1966.

Philo. *Philo: Volume 7*. Translated by F. H. Colson. LCL. Cambridge, MA: Harvard University Press, 1998.

Pitt-Rivers, Julian, editor. *Mediterranean Countrymen: Essays in the Social Anthropology of the Mediterranean*. Paris: Mouton, 1963.

———. "Honour and Social Status." In *Honour and Shame: The Values of Mediterranean Society*, 19–77. Edited by J. G. Peristiany. Chicago: University of Chicago Press, 1966.

———. *The Fate of Shechem, or, The Politics of Sex: Essays in the Anthropology of the Mediterranean*. Cambridge, MA: Cambridge University Press, 1977.

Plummer, Alfred. *An Exegetical Commentary on the Gospel according to S. Matthew*. London: Robert Scott, 1928.

Plutarch. *Lives: Demosthenes and Cicero; Alexander and Caesar*. Translated by Bernadotte Perrin. LCL. Cambridge, MA: Harvard University Press, 1999.

Pomeroy, Sarah B. *Goddesses, Whores, Wives, and Slaves: Women in Classical Antiquity*. New York: Schoken, 1975.

Porter, Stanley E. *Handbook of Classical Rhetoric in the Hellenistic Period: 330 B.C.—A.D. 400*. Boston: Brill, 2001.

Prusher, Ilene R. "As Order Slides, Palestinian Women Face Honor Killings." *Christian Science Monitor*, 20 November 2007, World 1.

Qureshi, Tanveer. "The Deadly Ending to a 'Melodrama.'" *The Times*, 19 June 2007, Features/Law 1.

Rabinowitz, J. J. "Marriage Contracts in Ancient Egypt in the Light of Jewish Sources." *Harvard Theological Review* 46 (1953) 91–97.

Raif, Shenai. "Honour-Killing Victim Raped before Her Torture Death." *Birmingham Post*, 20 July 2007. News 2.

Rimmer, Alan. "Honour Killing Riddle of Knifed Girl, 17; Family Quizzed as Pregnant Wife Is Found at Home with Multiple Stab Wounds." *Mail on Sunday*, 13 May 2007, 10.

Robinson, Theodore. *The Gospel of Matthew*. London: Hodder and Stoughton, 1928.

Rohrbaugh, Richard L. "Introduction." In *The Social Sciences and New Testament Interpretation*, 1–15. Edited by Richard L. Rohrbaugh. Peabody, MA: Hendrickson, 1996.

Ruggi, Suzanne. "Honor Killings in Palestine: Commodifying Honor in Female Sexuality." *Middle East Report* 28.1 (1998) 12–15.

Rule, Andrew K. "Born of the Virgin Mary." *Christianity Today*, 7 December 1959, 3–5.

Saadawi, Nawal. *The Hidden Face of Eve*. Translated and edited by Sherif Hetata. London: Zed Press, 1980.

Sabir, Nadirah Z. "The Adventures of a Muslim Woman in Atlanta." In *Shattering the Stereotypes: Muslim Women Speak Out*, 127–41. Edited by Fawzia Afzal-Khan Northampton: Olive Branch, 2005.

Sahibjam, F. *The Stoning of Soraya*. New York: Arcade, 1994.

Scally, Derek. "Brother Gets Nine-Year Sentence for 'Honour Killing' of Sister." *Irish Times*, 14 April 2007, World 9.

Schaberg, Jane. *The Illegitimacy of Jesus: A Feminist Theological Interpretation of the Infancy Narratives*. New York: Harper & Row, 1987.

Schneemelcher, Wilhelm, editor. *New Testament Apocrypha*, vol. 1, *Gospels and Related Writings*. Translated by R. McL. Wilson. Rev ed. Louisville: Westminster John Knox, 1991.

Schneider, Jane. "Of Vigilance and Virgins: Honor, Shame, and Access to Resources in Mediterranean Societies." *Ethnology* 10 (1971) 1–24.

Schweizer, Eduard. *The Good News according to Matthew*. Translated by David E. Green. London: SPCK, 1980.

Sev'er, A. *A Cross-Cultural Exploration of Wife Abuse: Problems and Prospectus*. Queenstown, NY: E. Mellen, 1997.

Shah, Hassam Qadir. *There Is No "Honour" in Killing: Don't Let Them Get Away with Murder*. Lahore: Shirkat Gah, 2002.

Simonetti, Manlio, editor. *Matthew 1–13*. Ancient Christian Commentary on Scripture, New Testament 1a. Downers Grove, IL: InterVarsity, 2001.

Smid, H. R. *Protevangelium Jacobi: A Commentary*. Apocrypha Novi Testamenti 1. Assen: Van Gorcum, 1965.

Smith, Lewis. "Muslim Killed Daughter for the 'Dishonour' of Having Boyfriend." *The Times*, 30 September 2003, News 5.

Smith, Robert H. *Matthew*. Augsburg Commentary on the New Testament. Minneapolis: Augsburg, 1989.

Souad, in collaboration with Marie-Thérèse Cuny. *Burned Alive: The Shocking, True Story of One Women's Escape from an 'Honour' Killing*. London: Bantam, 2004.

Stanton, Graham. *The Interpretation of Matthew*. Issues in Religion and Theology 3. Philadelphia: Fortress, 1983.

Stoil, Rebecca Anna. "Druse Woman Victim of Suspected Honor Killing." *Jerusalem Post*, 4 May 2006, News 2.

Strack, Hermann L., and Paul Billerbeck. *Das Evangelium Nach Matthäus Erläutert aus Talmud und Midrasch*. Kommentar zum Neuen Testament aus Talmud und Midrasch. Munich: Oskar Beck, 1922.

Swain, Jon. "My Family Killed My Sister: I Could Be Next." *Sunday Times*, 17 June 2007, Features 10.

Sweet, Louis Matthews. *The Birth and Infancy of Jesus Christ*. Philadelphia: Westminster. 1906.

Tanveer, Khalid. "Honour's Ghastly Tally." *Hobart Mercury*, 4 January 2006. In Depth 17.

Tatum, W. Barnes. "Origins of Jesus Messiah (Matt 1:1, 18a): Matthew's Use of the Infancy Traditions." *Journal of Biblical Literature* 96.4 (1977) 523–35.

Taylor, Jerome. "Love that Can Be Lethal: Muslim Couples in Fear of 'Honour' Killing." *The Independent*, 29 June 2007.

Taylor, Vincent. *The Historical Evidence for the Virgin Birth*. Oxford: Clarendon, 1920.

Thompson, Dave. *The Dark Reign of Gothic Rock: In the Reptile House with the Sisters of Mercy, Bauhaus, and the Cure*. London: Helter Skelter, 2002.

Tintori, Karen. *Unto the Daughters: The Legacy of an Honor Killing in a Sicilian-American Family*. New York: St. Martin's, 2007.

Tosato, Angelo. "Joseph, Being a Just Man (Matt 1:19)." *Catholic Biblical Quarterly* 41 (1979) 547–51.

Trilling, Wolfgang. *The Gospel according to St. Matthew*. Vol. 1 London: Burns & Oates, 1969.

Turner, H. E. W. "Expository Problems: The Virgin Birth." *Expository Times* 68.1 (1956) 12–17.

Twomey, John. "Mother-In-Law, 70, will Die in Jail for Bride's Honour Killing." *The Express*, 20 September 2007, News 31.

Van Aarde, Andries G. "The Evangelium infantium, the abandonment of children, and the infancy narrative in Matthew 1 and 2 from a social-scientific perspective." *Society of Biblical Literature Seminary Papers* 31 (1992) 435–53.

Verma, Sonia. "Miss Israel Finalist Quits after Family's Honour Killing Plot." *The Times*, 9 March 2007, News 35.

Walsh, Declan. "'We Feel No Shame'—The Brothers Who Killed their Sister for Honour: Tragic Tale Highlights Scale of Beatings and Murder of Women in Countryside." *The Guardian*, 7 February 2007, International 23.

Ward, David. "Sikh Wife's Affair Sparks Honour Killing by Husband and His Mother." *The Guardian*, 3 May 2007, Home 4.

Warnock, Kitty. *Land before Honour: Palestinian Women in the Occupied Territories*. New York: Monthly Review Press, 1990.

Wells, Bruce. "Sex, Lies, and Virginal Rape: The Slandered Bride and False Accusations in Deuteronomy." *Journal of Biblical Literature* 124.1 (2005) 41–72.

Weren, Wim J. C. "The Five Women and Matthew's Genealogy." *Catholic Biblical Quarterly* 59 (1997) 288–305.

Westbook, Raymond. *Old Babylonian Marriage Law*. Horn: Berger & Söhne, 1988.

Wharton, Jane. "Stoned to Death as 1,000 Villagers Take Pictures. . . . Her Crime? Loving a Man from the Wrong Religion." *The Express*, 4 May 2007, News 17.

Wikan, Unni. "Shame and Honor: A Contestable Pair." *Man* 19.4 (1984) 635–52.

———. *In Honor of Fadime: Murder and Shame*. Rev. ed. Chicago: University of Chicago Press, 2008.

Witherington, Ben. *Women in the Earliest Churches*. Cambridge, MA: Cambridge University Press, 1988.

Zervos, G. "Dating the Protevangelium of James: The Justin Martyr Connection." In *Society of Biblical Literature 1994 Seminar Papers*, 415–34. Edited by E. Lovering. Atlanta: Scholars, 1994.

Zoepf, Katherine. "25% of Wives in Syria are Abused, UN Study Finds." *International Herald Tribune*, 12 April 2006, News 5.

14857979R00065

Made in the USA
San Bernardino, CA
10 September 2014